# The Not So Solid South

*Anthropological Studies in a*
*Regional Subculture*

# The Not So Solid South

*Anthropological Studies in a Regional Subculture*

J. KENNETH MORLAND, Editor

*Southern Anthropological Society Proceedings, No. 4*

SOUTHERN ANTHROPOLOGICAL SOCIETY
Distributed by University of Georgia Press
Athens, 30601

# SOUTHERN ANTHROPOLOGICAL SOCIETY

Founded 1966

*Officers 1970-71*

Copyright © 1971 by
Southern Anthropological Society
LC 70-1429122
ISBN 8203-0304-6
Printed in the United States

# Contents

# Preface

WITH the publication of this volume the Southern Anthropologica Society inaugurates two changes in its program of publication. One change is to a more compact and more attractive format, and the other change is in the number of Proceedings published. The Society will continue its established policy of publishing a Proceedings each year consisting of papers presented at the "key symposium" of each annual spring meeting. The innovation is that when funds permit the Society will publish additional Proceedings numbered consecutively with the others. Like the present volume, these additional Proceedings will usually consist of collections of papers dealing with a particular subject or problem. The papers in this collection were selected from those presented at recent American Anthropological Association and Southern Anthropological Society meetings and from a conference sponsored by the Center for Southern Studies at Duke University. However, this need not be the case in the future: the policy will remain flexible, and other kinds of manuscripts will be considered. This collection, *The Not So Solid South*, is an appropriate beginning for this new program of publication. In an era in which college students are questioning the relevance of anthropology to contemporary society, the papers in this collection show in a rather direct fashion how anthropology can be not only relevant but readable.

This volume owes much to the editorial criticism of my wife, Joyce Rockwood Hudson.

Charles Hudson
SAS Editor

# Introduction

J. KENNETH MORLAND

AT the 68th Annual Meeting of the American Anthropological Association in New Orleans in November, 1969, one of the resolutions presented to the membership called for support of anthropological studies of American society. Overwhelmingly approved, the resolution stated:

> Whereas anthropological studies of contemporary American society are essential to the advancement of anthropology as a science and to the well being of the society,
> And whereas increasing numbers of students entering anthropology wish to undertake research on contemporary American society,
> And whereas such studies, and the training of students to undertake them, have been relatively neglected,
> Therefore,
> Be it resolved that the American Anthropological Association recognizes the legitimacy and importance of such research and training, and urges the active development of both.

Actually, the papers included in this volume anticipated the resolution, for they are anthropological studies of American society that were well under way prior to November, 1969. Most of the papers were selected from those presented in a symposium on the American South at the annual meeting of the Southern Anthropological Society in March, 1969, and from another symposium on the same topic at the 68th Annual Meeting of the American Anthropological Association. In addition, two were first presented at a conference sponsored by the Center for Southern Studies at Duke University in January, 1969.

The papers in this volume are significant for several reasons. First, they demonstrate a considerable range of possibilities for

1

anthropological research in present-day American society, particularly in the South. They deal with such varied groups as a healing sect, gypsies, coal miners, peasants, urban mill workers, moonshiners, a hippie ghetto, and a remnant Indian tribe; and with such cultural phenomena as pottery traditions, funeral practices, religious disease, and techniques for eluding the sheriff. They are therefore suggestive of the kinds of projects close at hand that may be utilized in the training of graduate students and as the objects of field work by seasoned anthropologists. These research undertakings show that it is not always necessary for anthropologists to go to remote places or to find exotic peoples in order to do research.

Second, these research papers illustrate the complexity of the Southern regional subculture. They show that the South is far from being as homogeneous or "solid" as it has sometimes been called. It is to be noted that these studies are termed research *in* rather than *of* the region, for there is no pretense that they represent the study of the South as a whole. Indeed, some might say that the groups dealt with in these papers are not in the mainstream of the regional sub-culture, and that their very differences and relative isolation make them amenable to anthropological research. All we can say at this point is that these groups do exist in the South and are presumably part of the regional subculture. The papers are offered as beginnings of what might be extensive anthropological research to establish just what is held in common by Southerners. It is true that at least three of the studies point to regional subcultural characteristics: Crocker's "The Southern Way of Death," Peacock's "The Southern Protestant Ethic Disease," and Sayers' "The Southern Pottery Tradition"; and most of the other studies imply characteristics that appear to permeate the region. However, these regional generalizations are stated as hypotheses that require testing through further research.

Third, these research undertakings demonstrate that participant-observation, the hallmark of anthropological method, can be employed in the culture of which the researcher is a part. It is evident that the groups described in these papers have been observed and analyzed with objectivity and that the cultural background of the researchers has not hindered their perception. At the same time, they have realized one great advantage from studying within their own culture, namely the understanding of the language, making it unnecessary to resort to interpreters. Admittedly, these studies cannot hope to succeed fully in being "holistic," that is, in being related to the entire society and culture of which the group or phenomenon studied is a part. When anthropologists do research on relatively small, isolated, homogeneous societies, the problem of showing the inter-relatedness of culture patterns is not so great. With a large, hetero-geneous society, however, trying to deal with the cultural context of the behavior being described and analyzed is difficult indeed. Nevertheless, it is something with which the anthropologist must deal if his study of American society and culture is to be successful. More will be said about this in the concluding chapter. In addition to the use of anthropological method, it is to be noted that the authors of these studies apply to American society concepts developed in tra-ditional anthropological study of smaller, more homogeneous folk societies. Thus, one of the papers employs "rites of passage" and "revitalization process," two deal with "peasantry," and another relies on "symbolic behavior" as an organizing concept. The assumption is that American society is as amenable to the use of such terms as any other society.

Fourth, it is significant that most of the contributors to this volume are relatively young. Some have only recently acquired their graduate degrees, and some are still in the process of doing so. In accord with the resolution of the American Anthropological Association calling for more studies of American society, these authors represent a con-siderable number of anthropologists who at the very beginning of their careers share a strong interest in increasing the understanding of their own culture through anthropological research. Anthropologists have much to learn about American society and culture, and with many younger anthropologists showing strong interest the future of the research necessary to such learning is bright.

The papers are arranged so that studies of specific groups precede studies that look at aspects of behavior which are assumed to charac-terize the South as a whole. Once more, it is to be emphasized that the authors of these research reports present highly tentative gen-eralizations about what they have studied. The papers are offered as starting points of what the authors hope will lead to more extensive research by themselves and by others.

All of the contributors, including the editor, are especially in-debted to Charles Hudson, Proceedings editor, for his encourage-ment, helpful suggestions, and skillful guidance of this volume into print.

# Higher on the Hog

HELEN PHILLIPS KEBER

THE following pages are an attempt to substantiate the position that black divine healing in a southeastern United States town does not pose a barrier to sociocultural change but rather encourages such change among its members. I have conducted research on a group of black divine healers in Oakboro from May 1968 continuously to the present.[1] Oakboro, located in the Piedmont of the Appalachians, is composed of three major social segments—low-income whites, the blacks, and university personnel and students. The group I have been studying is numerically small. Those in regular attendance at the weekly healing meeting include about eleven women, ten men, and their children. A few others come less regularly. It is entirely a volunteer group and forms only a small portion of the black community of which it is a part. The leader is a black woman, Sister Thompson, from another town, who leaves her family every weekend to come to Oakboro. Every Friday night she holds a healing meeting in the home of one of the "Saints," the term by which I shall refer to Sister Thompson and her followers. During the rest of the weekend she spends the nights in the Saints' homes, has the members come visit with her to discuss their problems, goes shopping with them, and, in general participates in their activities. She is essential to the group; without her it would disband.

There is little agreement upon the best label for, and by implication the best way to conceive of, the sociocultural situation of the Saints.[2] Whether to term it lower-class culture (Frazier 1966), a culture of poverty after Oscar Lewis (1966), an American subculture or subsociety, or black culture *per se* (Keil 1966) is currently debated because it is an issue that is both central to research and to methodological and theoretical orientations. Terming the Saints low-income blacks is appropriate in one sense; yet it suggests similarities with blacks throughout the United States that I have not found to be valid (Young 1970). My solution is to utilize an approach appropriate for delimiting sociocultural variables in developing nations. The Saints are definitely responding to sociocultural change which is best characterized as a shift from a more "traditional" life—farm-reared, white-dominated—into a more "modern" one—dependence on cash, the securing of material goods, and the development of a self-image as equal to whites. The following paragraphs outline some aspects of this change.

Sister Thompson and the Saints are confronted with the surrounding society's many specialized organizations and institutions. They must adapt to some of these; others they ignore or avoid. Hence, the degree to which they participate in this surrounding society must be investigated.

Compared to United States society as a whole, the Saints are poorly educated. The adults themselves have in no case completed high school, all having grown up on farms and moved to town as adults. However, their children are being sent through the school system.

The Saints possess skills which are unspecialized in comparison with those of many people in the United States. All utilize the same skill—menial or manual labor—in a variety of jobs. The men work as janitors at the university, at a grocery store, or at the Town Hall. The women work as maids in private homes, in schools, or in businesses. With this same unspecialized skill they can and have worked in a variety of jobs. Their employment periodically shifts, especially in the case of the women. Basically, obtainment of jobs follows the modernized pattern of universalism; i.e., obtainment of jobs is based on ability rather than on ascribed status. Referral is by word-of-mouth or by formal application and is not handed from kin to kin or gained through "pull." Nevertheless, in one important aspect obtainment of jobs is particularistic. They obtain these jobs by being who they are—by being black.

Politics, whether local, state, or national, is a topic I have rarely heard mentioned, despite admiration for both Martin Luther King, Jr. and the Kennedys. The racial riots are viewed as an effective political instrument, but the Christian outlook of the Saints leads them to disagree with violence as a means to an end. In their opinion one should act with love towards all one's fellow men, yet they believe the riots brought about changes which King and other peaceful civil rights workers were unable to accomplish. Occasionally they talk of formulating a petition to have their dirt roads paved. Such talk is closer to overt political action than anything I have encountered. Even in the November 1968 local, state, and national elections not one of the members voted, despite a suspicion that if Nixon were elected it would be detrimental to blacks.

The Saints participate in formalized churches with the encouragement of Sister Thompson but with the warning that not all ministers are honest and sincere. Their churches appear to be a potent factor in their adjustment to modern life. For one thing, the minister of the largest black church in town, and the one to which the majority of the Saints belong, is a civic leader in addition to being a religious leader. In both capacities he is involved in many committees and other community activities. As their leader he provides his congregation with a model after which they expect to pattern their lives. The bureaucratic nature of his activities provides for his congregation a role model that is not a part of their "traditional" life.

In addition to the minister's role, the structure of the formalized church offers its congregation an experience in modern living. Based on state and national church institutions, many committees and organizations in which the members participate compose the structure of the church. Rather than conducting solely business meetings, their meetings take the broad form of a church service interrupted for the business sessions which substitute for the sermon and are conducted by parliamentary procedure. My contention is that familiarity with the existence of these church organizations and with their manner of operation provides the members with a means of comprehending and handling the many specialized organizations, including bureaucratic systems, which they encounter in their surrounding society, a means which again is not in evidence in other aspects of the life of the Saints.

Kinship among blacks is a difficult subject with which to deal. Keil's characterization of black kinship as a battle of the sexes is manifest in the kinship of the Saints. Their marriages are more permanent than those that Keil (1966) and Liebow (1967) describe for the ghetto. The men stay with their families, perhaps because they are able to obtain regular employment and are thereby encouraged to "sink roots into the world in which they live" (Liebow 1967:70). Nevertheless, relationships between the sexes appear to be governed by what Keil terms "variations of the finance-romance equation" (Keil 1966:9) rather than by a concern for the primacy of the nuclear family. The men do not fit the white middle-class husband's role of provider; rather they aspire to the role of their culture hero—the hustler, the good preacher, or the entertainer who is financially well-off without having to undergo regular work for an employer. With no loss of respect to the husband, the wife contributes as much to the cash income as he does, if not more, regardless of whether they have children to support.

With this brief entrance into the lives of the Saints, I will now turn attention to their Friday night healing meeting. I will attempt to convey to the reader the experience of the Friday night meeting through a description in print. The medium of print is, however, ironically unsuited to this purpose. Most of white America reveres the printed word, the literary tradition, and its attendant values. On the other hand, among the Saints the spoken word and the oral tradition carry more power. Their modes of perception and expression and their channels of communication are primarily auditory and tactile rather than visual and literate (Keil 1966:16-7). It is essential in the description which follows to pay attention to the auditory and tactile activities of the healing meeting rather than to view the description as a transcription of a hypothetical meeting.

There are three parts to the healing meetings: the devotional, the testimonial, and the healing. The healing meeting is unlike many middle-class, white liturgical church services for which a printed program maps beforehand in minute detail the order, the content, and the form of the many parts. In the healing meeting the boundaries between the three parts are only sometimes enunciated and clear cut. At other times one part flows into the other or the testimonials and the healing may become intertwined. Not only are the boundaries indefinite but the procedure and the outcome are not planned beforehand. The boundaries remain fluid as the members respond to Sister Thompson, to one another, and to the Holy Spirit within themselves.

The setting is a house of one of the members. Some houses are large enough to comfortably accommodate everyone; others are small, so that everyone is crowded together with the children on each other's or an adult's lap. Even in the heat of summer the doors and windows are closed and the drapes drawn, although strangers are welcomed. Not only does this prevent the devils who are upon the earth from using what goes on during the service to their own evil ends, but it also prevents distractions from outside the circle in which everyone is seated.

The members arrive and enter the living room around eight o'clock at night. Rather than assuming a reverent attitude, they talk with one another, discussing the cars outside, what went on last week, the dog next door, the milkman, or joke with each other, or watch television. Sister Thompson goes into the back bedroom where the people may follow to talk with her. Perhaps someone starts a song.

Perhaps Sister Thompson reappears, asking someone to read the scripture and lead the prayer, the events which constitute the devotional. Usually it is a group prayer, signaled by the phrase, "Let every heart in the building pray," so that everyone gets down on his knees and addresses the Lord directly. In this short and informal manner the stage is set for the rest of the evening.

Usually somewhere near the beginning Sister Thompson will stand up and take over leadership by announcing that the service is open to testimony. She says: "Let every heart sing, pray, dance, do whatever the Spirit leads you to do. If the Spirit says 'Shout,' you shout. If it says, 'Sing,' you sing. Let's not clap our hands lightly and half-heartedly, but loudly and from our hearts. And stomp your feet. If you do, it won't be long until you are out there shouting for the Lord."

She encourages, cajoles, coaxes, and reprimands the members into participating not only with their spoken testimonies but with their entire bodies.

The testimonial is directed towards praising the Lord. It is not a confession of sins. The several attempts at turning it into confession that I witnessed were unsuccessful and unapproved. Everyone is patient with a confession, since one direction of the meeting is that everyone always—within the limits of what is considered moral—gets to do and is encouraged to do what he wants. Yet, after a confession, Sister Thompson will say, "Let's not confess our sins. Let's praise the Lord. Let's tell what the Lord has done for us. The Lord has done so many things. Let's praise his name." Thus, the testimonial is a praising of the Lord, a listing of blessings received. It is an activity in which everyone present must participate.

The general pattern is to begin one's testimony with a song. One person will begin the song and lead it, although leadership may be taken over by someone else at any time during the song. When the song is well underway (and it can go on as long as is wanted) the individual who started it stands up. He testifies, usually relating the first part of his testimony to the theme of the song. The rest of the testimony may continue on an entirely different tangent. A person can give a short, formalized testimony or a long, personal testimony. Sometimes the long testimonies actually become narrative story-telling, as when one individual recounted all the events of his long trip to and from California. Or a person can simply list all the things which the Lord has done for him. The individual may also lead a prayer in his testimony.

The testimonies are earthy and mundane, bringing to mind daily, non-ritual life with its struggles and conflicts, its good and bad sides, its miracles and simple happenings, its successes and hopes. Sometimes they are monotonous and ticked off mechanically; but then again they are told with enthusiasm and fervor so that everyone responds with "Amen, Yes Sir, Tell it like it is," with a clapping of hands to the rhythmical rhetoric or with shouting. If the individual becomes so enwrapped in his testimony that it is obvious the Lord is going to bless him at that moment instead of during the healing, Sister Thompson will take the lead, starting a song which everyone takes up while the individual dances and shouts, rejoicing in his contact with the Lord.

Usually near the beginning—although she may do this more than once—Sister Thompson gives a testimony which approaches being a sermon. It is impromptu, for written speeches are not considered to be the Lord's words. Sister Thompson tells the Saints how to live by giving examples of how the Lord has told her to live. Yet the members may revere her words not so much from the logic of what she says as from the manner in which she tells it. Keil writes regarding blue-singers that "It is the intensity and conviction with which the story is spelled out, the fragments of experience pieced together, rather than the story itself" (1966:17) by which performances are measured. The same may be true of Sister Thompson's testimony. It is usually long, with no central theme but with many subjects, the fragment of one leading to a related other. Her approach to validation is a frenzied one. She will lull through an extended interval with side-stories and occasional jokes. But when she reaches her point, her voice becomes louder, her emphases stronger, she repeats phrases, and slides into a rhythmical rhetoric which borders on being a song. She leads, clapping at the end of each phrase and tapping her foot throughout; the members form the chorus, affirming her every phrase through their hands, feet, and voices. As a leader her sense of timing is superb. She knows how to phrase, when to pause, where to accent, how to hold and bend a word, a note, or her body.

The climax of the meeting does not come until the healing. The point of it is to receive a blessing from the Lord. That is what the members say they come for and why participation is encouraged. The blessing comes when Sister Thompson lays her hands on the individual, thereby transferring the power of the Lord which resides in her to the individual and taking on any demons that may be in his body. It is a tactile experience, for the individual feels the power, the spirit of the Lord, move through his body. The Saints say it is similar to an electric shock.

Sister Thompson might pray over each individual as all stand in a circle. She might make them form a long line or form several lines, each having a special purpose. Sometimes she simply says one prayer that applies to everyone. Sometimes she has each person approach her. As everyone touches a part of her body, she bends and sways. Sometimes blessings are obtained by touching her hands as the olive oil with which she has been anointed runs down her arms. Sometimes she has everyone place their purses and wallets or their shoes in a pile and she says a blessing over them.

During the healing there is much support and participation from those who are not being prayed over at the moment. Everyone will be singing, shouting, and clapping. Someone will have started a song, in which everyone joins. Usually the song is fast-moving with only one or two lines that are repeated again and again and again. With repetition the bodily movements, the clapping, and the foot-tapping require less and less effort as they flow with the music. Usually the same song continues throughout the healing; occasionally it is changed. Sometimes there is a leader, sometimes there is not. People clap, tap their feet, shout, suddenly dance and get into frenzies, which are outside the song and the beat; and people pass out in a trance on the floor. A beat permeates the atmosphere, the floor sends it through one's feet, the chairs reverberate, the clapping encourages it, the song can not break from it, the rise and fall singsong of those praying is formed by it. The praying is a request for a blessing made by Sister Thompson for the individual she is praying over. Each request has the same rhythmical refrain; they are matched. The request begins on a high note from which she glides down about three or four notes to a level on which her vibrato sustains and draws out the prayer. Lorrine and Jack, her assistants, carry on their own singsong which they synchronize to fit that of Sister Thompson. Theirs, each of which is different, are not identical to hers but fit the same rhythm, so that the prayer becomes a trio. The shouts of "Glory, hallelujah," "Amen," "Yes, Jesus," are caught in the beat of the song and the trio. As Sister Thompson reaches the pinnacle of her request, she grippingly lays on her hands; the individual jolts as the "electric shock" of his blessing from the Lord shoots through him, while the beat and the song endure.

The rest of the meeting is anticlimactical. An informal atmosphere with small talk among various members pervades the offering and its blessing. There is a request for any additional remarks (in which members who were late or did not get to testify can do so), for announcements, for telling about a particularly good blessing received during the healing, followed by the benediction and the farewell handshaking.

The healing meeting encourages the members to new behavior in their daily lives rather than encouraging them to continue in a subordinate relation to whites or strengthening their attachment to "traditional" life. To understand the meeting as such it is necessary to view the ritual as action and form rather than as the mapping out of an ideology. The final paragraphs suggest the processes by which participation in the healing meeting offers an effective means of coping with modern life.

When I meet one of the Saints the day after, or several days after the Friday night meeting, or when I overhear several of them discussing the meeting, talk always centers on how "good" the meeting was. If a person was not there, his first question will be, "Was it a good meeting?" If he was there, he will begin the discussion by declaring "Wasn't it a good meeting!" "Good" meetings are desired and some meetings are "better" than others. The Saints say they are "out to have a good time in the Lord" at the meeting; they are there "to enjoy" themselves. Yet, "good" meetings do not just happen. They occur when the spirit is high. A high spirit is created in the following manner.

As I noted above, Sister Thompson usually gives a testimony early in the meeting, shortly after the devotional. In it she encourages everyone to participate vigorously, explaining to them all the ways that one can "make a joyful noise to the Lord" and reminding them that if they participate "from the heart," they will soon be filled with the Lord—i.e., obtain a blessing. She also testifies to the many blessings she has received, thereby pointing out the wide range in their testimonies, drawing from all sorts of daily experiences, to make their testimonies intimate, creative, and insightful rather than rattling off a string of formalities. If encouragement is not enough, when the individual finishes his testimony Sister Thompson will often require him to stand up again and tell such-and-such a tale to the glory of God. She is very concerned that the spirit of the meeting not be broken. The only instances in which I have seen her interrupt the service is to give this instruction. Her efforts to elicit meaningful testimonies are efforts to raise the spirit, to create a "good" meeting. A meaningful testimony includes references to gaining that which is desired—health, money, clothes, houses, cars, tires, food, employment, a saved spouse, the outwitting of a policeman, a safe journey, an equitable outcome in a struggle with an employer. As opposed to confessing one's sins, bemoaning how miserable the world is, monotonously rattling off formalities, bringing up these successes evokes excitement in the others because they seek gratification in similar successes. They can identify with the conflict and vicariously enjoy the outcome. Their excitement is manifest in the animation during meaningful testimonies—in the responses from the others and, if the teller's enthusiasm is great enough, in the occasional outburst into song, dancing, clapping, tapping, and shouting during the testimony instead of during the healing. A meaningful testimony elicits more animation just as enthusiastic singing with accompanying loud clapping and hard and rapid foot tapping does between testimonies. Also, greater activity in singing leads to more sincere testimonies and vice versa. The more animation, the greater is the spirit, and, hence, the better is the meeting.

Participation seems to breed more participation. Yet the structure of the testimony is extremely fluid. A testimony inciting the members to action may be followed by a stirring song, but the next four or five testimonies may be formalities and the songs limp. Sister Thompson may stand up and give another talk or begin and lead a propelling song. It is in essence the last chance to create a high spirit verbally before the healing. As does the testimony in general, her talk consists of a series of highs and lows in spirit but tends before the end to develop into rhythmical rhetoric with much participation from the group. Thus, a rise and fall in the amount of participation and involvement by the members, a rise and fall in the degree of spirit, punctuates the testimony. In order to sustain a generally high level of spirit throughout, individual effort must be put into the testimonies and the songs.

The testimony contributes much to the healing. Throughout the healing the spirit is on a much higher level than it was during the testimony. If the meeting is a "good" one, the contrast between the testimony and the healing in intensity of spirit is much greater than when the meeting is "poor." A "poor" meeting is characterized by having approximately the same—generally, low—level throughout. Thus, the more the testimony creates a high spirit, the greater is the likelihood of a high spirit during the healing.

Besides the influence of the testimonial, another factor heightening the spirit during the healing is the degree to which individuals act upon the spirit as it enters their bodies. If one individual goes into a frenzy, others are likely to follow suit. If another starts beating the tambourine rapidly, the others will clap harder. If someone begins dancing and continues unable to get the satisfaction of his blessing, the others will stomp their feet until the floor sways with the beat. In a "good" meeting, participation does indeed breed participation, for the more one person acts out his blessing, the more others will act out theirs, and the more still others will contribute to the singing, clapping, and stamping. These, in turn, move someone to be more active in receiving his blessing. In a "good" meeting, the members participate to a greater extent and more intensely during the healing.

The healing is the climax of the meeting, for it is both the point of greatest participation—everyone acting in unison to the beat for a prolonged period of time—and the time for consummating the participants' goal in coming to the meeting—i.e., receiving a blessing. When a "good" meeting is created with a high spirit throughout the healing, the chances are better for many individuals to consummate their goal, to receive a blessing.

To be rational is to have a goal in mind for which one is willing to change his behavior in order to attain it. I would argue that the healing service encourages the members to act rationally to attain their goal, the blessing. In order to attain it they must change their means of attaining a blessing; means which include participation in the testimonies, the songs, and the healing. They must strive to delve into their daily lives and interpret situations through the framework of God's rules during the testimony and they must strive to put more effort into the singing, dancing, shouting, clapping, and tapping. Too, the individual must learn to adjust himself to a delayed gratification before attaining his goal. He requests the blessing during his testimony and must wait for his chance to receive a blessing through the lulls of the meeting, through others' testimonies, through the songs, through Sister Thompson's sermon, and while others before him are being prayed over. Finally, when his chance comes, he must struggle to dispel the devil that is within him and that causes him to resist, allowing the spirit to enter his body. The healing meeting thus provides the individual with a goal and with a means of attaining it, but with a means that involves changing his attitudes and behavior towards more constructive participation.

Rationality, it can be argued, is necessary for successful adjustment to modernized society. By necessity and by choice the Saints have become and are becoming more dependent on their surrounding society. They no longer grow most of their food as they did on the farm, either to consume or to sell for cash. Instead they rely on their menial services in jobs controlled by their employers. Cars, telephones, clothes, refrigerators, stoves, and houses are necessary for existence in modern society. Yet the Saints' means of attaining them are limited. By choice they desire a comfortable house, reliable car, an education for their children, a television set, employment which would not be so utterly dependent on their employer's whims, a free choice of food, and self-respect. Recent civil rights legislation has served to reinforce their desire for the fruits of modern society and has encouraged them to feel it is their right to attain them. Yet it has been the position of the black in the United States to "stay in his place," to accept his lot without trying to change it, to feel he is a second-class citizen with no other alternative, and to feel lucky to have a shack, a run-down car, hand-me-down clothes, or "kind" employers. In other words, there is a discrepancy now between what the Saints found to be true of life in the past and hints of what life could be in the future. Sister Thompson encourages her followers to believe in the hints, to act in a free and equal manner, and to participate in modern life— to buy a car, a house, obtain a better job, and so forth. Nevertheless, legislation only paves the road. A means of traveling over it is also necessary. It is not enough to feel that one has a right to modern life and to want to participate in it. One must also be willing to find a means and to change his life by utilizing the means. One must plan for the future and be able to cope with delayed gratification, struggles, and striving in order to attain one's goal.

I have argued that Sister Thompson's healing meeting encourages utilization of one's means and this kind of coping. However, it not only encourages such coping, but also paints the process of coping as a desired and joyful process with its bright sides and rewards. Moreover, the outcome of the process of coping—the blessing—is not limited to a religious ceremony or to religious action. Rather, it is the promise of a success in daily life.

It is during the meeting when the Spirit is high and God is within their bodies that the attitude of equality as brothers under God is made emphatic, that problems in changing their lives are made clear, that resolutions are proposed, and that they are taught the means to participate actively in solving their problems. Thus, the prospect of a different future is opened and planning for it encouraged. It is then that they say:

> If you go into a grocery store and you see a steak and you want that steak, then you buy it. God didn't put steak on the earth just for the rich people. He put it there for His people. It's time we quit eating chitterlings and hog's feet and moved higher on the hog.[3]

## NOTES

1. My entrée as a white into the black group came by a 'Godsend.' Before I knew anything of Sister Thompson or the Saints, I had become interested in a Church of God campgrounds close to Oakboro. A friend introduced me to his black maid whom he knew to be religiously inclined, in order that I might learn about the campgrounds. When I told her I wished to study divine healing, long discussions ensued. The maid, a Baptist, had little to do with the campgrounds, but was eager to discuss the merits of various divine healers and the effectiveness of divine healing. She found that my interest was sincere and noted that as a college graduate I could read and write well. While not a healer herself, to serve the Lord she held small evening gatherings during which she read and fathomed the meaning of the Bible. Because she reads and writes slowly and has never learned many Biblical words, she had been praying to the Lord for someone to assist her, so that she might better accomplish His work. Obviously to her, I had been sent by the Lord as His answer. Her account of this story when introducing me to Sister Thompson, the Saints, and others in the community explained the anomaly of my being with her, as well as establishing my interest in divine healing. Sister Thompson, the Saints, and the town have been given fictitious names.

2. See Valentine (1969) for a synopsis of implications of various labels.

3. In my experience, the Saints eat as little of chitterlings and hog's feet as they do of steak (virtually none). They choose other foods over steak, given comparable amounts of money. Sister Thompson's use of these terms in the concluding statement may thus be interpreted as expressing symbolically the desirability of adopting modern ways and putting aside traditional ways.

## REFERENCES

Frazier, E. Franklin, 1966. *The Negro Family in the United States* (Chicago: University of Chicago Press). First published in 1932.

Keil, Charles, 1966. *Urban Blues* (Chicago: University of Chicago Press).

Lewis, Oscar, 1966. *La Vida* (New York: Random House).

Liebow, Elliott, 1967. *Tally's Corner: a Study of Negro Street-cornermen* (Boston: Little, Brown, and Company).

Valentine, Charles A., 1969. Culture and Poverty: Critique and Counter-Proposals. *Current Anthropology* 10:181-201.

Young, Virginia Heyer, 1970. Family and Childhood in a Southern Negro Community. *American Anthropologist* 72:269-288.

# "Gypsy" Research in the South

Jared Harper

One group of people largely neglected by anthropologists interested in Southern studies, or for that matter, by anthropologists in general, are the gypsies. Many articles on gypsies have appeared in the popular press, but to my knowledge there have been only two articles on gypsies appearing in anthropological journals, and neither of them is about gypsies in the South. One appeared in the *American Anthropologist* (Bonos 1942), while the second, a sequel to the first, appeared in the *Southwestern Journal of Anthropology* (Çoker 1966). Publications on gypsies in the South are limited to a few articles in popular magazines, religious periodicals, newspapers, and in a little known, non-anthropological, specialist journal. Of these, only three are worthy of note, consisting of one article each in *Reader's Digest* (Muller 1941), the *Journal of the Gypsy Lore Society* (Boles and Boles 1959), and in *Ave Maria* (Ryan 1967). We should not, however, overlook the recent papers by Harper (1968; 1969a; 1969b) and Harper and Hudson (1971; n.d.). The dearth of professional literature on gypsies and gypsies in the South in particular seems incredible since there are, I would estimate, from fifteen to twenty thousand people in the South alone labeled "gypsy" by the layman and perhaps from three to four times that number in the United States as a whole. These belong to four fairly distinct groups: the classical or Continental European Gypsies, the English Gypsies, the Scottish Gypsies, and the Irish Travelers, these being only general categories, each with several subgroups. Yet, despite the lack of professional literature on these groups, there are indications that any of them would provide a veritable storehouse of anthropological data relevant to the linguist, the ethnographer, the ethnomusicologist, or any other anthropological specialists.

THE IRISH TRAVELERS

My own Southern gypsy research has placed me in contact with one of these four groups—the Irish Travelers. Field work, so far, has been limited to only one Irish Traveler community numbering approximately twelve hundred people.[1] Entrée into the community was gained through a Catholic Father who served for nearly twenty years as their pastor and priest. It cannot be overemphasized that without his initial endorsement and support I could never have broken through the barrier of suspicion the Irish Travelers have built between themselves and outsiders. With his help I assumed the role of historian, there to write a history of the Irish Travelers. Similar barriers, no doubt, would be encountered by anyone attempting re search with any of the so-called Southern "gypsy" groups, although such barriers are by no means insurmountable, as I have shown.

Because of a lack of available quarters in the community I was studying, it was necessary for me to rent quarters about ten miles away and to commute from there to the community. This hampered my research somewhat but did not prove to be a major barrier. My field technique consisted primarily of participant observation and interviewing. I found that many informants were unwilling to record on tape, fearing that I would, perhaps, use the recordings to inflict harm upon them, although the same informants were perfectly willing for me to write down verbatim everything they said. Most informants even showed concern if it did not seem to them that I was writing fast enough to record all their statements.

Of the four gypsy groups mentioned earlier, the Irish Travelers seem to have played the largest part in the economic and social history of the rural South. Like the Yankee Peddler who supplied rural Southerners with the industrial products of the North, the Irish Travelers, too, served as middlemen, furnishing the Southern farmer with the mules so essential to his agricultural economy. Farmers who could not make the trek to one of the large Southern stock centers such as Memphis, Nashville, or Atlanta to purchase draft animals for their farms depended instead upon the itinerant Irish Traveler mule traders to come year after year "sellin' 'em and tradin' 'em," supplying the farmers with stock to carry them through planting and the harvest.

The Travelers, as they are commonly known, and it is the collective name which they themselves prefer, are not Romany Gypsies as are the members of the other three groups mentioned earlier, but are of Irish Stock. In fact, among the Irish Travelers "gypsy" is a fighting word, indeed many a fight has started between a Traveler and non-Traveler or "Country Person," as non-Travelers are called, when the latter inadvertently used "gypsy" as a term of reference. According to Traveler tradition, they emigrated from Ireland about 1847, during the Irish Potato Famine, driven to a better life in America by hunger and disease. Upon their arrival in America, so the Travelers say, the immigrants settled first in upstate New York, near Buffalo; near Pittsburgh and Germantown, Pennsylvania; and near Washington, D. C.

In Ireland, the Travelers were commonly known as "tinkers," although according to Patrick Greene this was somewhat of a misnomer since they performed any number of other itinerant occupations such as chimney sweeping, selling knick-knacks, clothespins, and baskets (usually handmade), swapping livestock, and as the occasion demanded they relied on petty swindling, thievery, and begging (Greene 1933-34:262). They traveled about the countryside with cart and horse living in tents and in the open air (Greene 1933-34:259-63). It might be said, however, that despite their Irish beginnings, the Travelers today seem to retain little that might be identified as Irish.

About the time of the American Civil War, my informants state, they abandoned all other occupations, moved to the South, and specialized in the mule and horse trade until about 1955 when that business virtually ceased. In those days boys learned the trade from their fathers by accompanying them on their trading forays into the countryside, a form of occupational training used by the Travelers today. They camped by the roadside in a friendly farmer's field, living in wagons and tents, and in later years in house trailers. Marriage was only within the group—arranged by the parents—a custom that continues to be practiced today and which shows no signs of changing. The Travelers of today practice uxorilocal residence after marriage, and this too is probably an old pattern.

At present, the Travelers live in several permanent and semipermanent communities in Georgia, South Carolina, Mississippi, Louisiana, Texas, and Tennessee, numbering about five thousand—a rough estimate. Their way of life has changed somewhat since the mule trading days, which many Travelers look back upon with nostalgia as the "good old days." As a rule only the men travel today, while the women and children remain at home in modern house trailers. This has been necessitated in part by their living in large mobile homes which are difficult and expensive to move. Also the cost of living on the road and compulsory school attendance laws are major factors in their traveling less.

Since the demise of the mule trade the Travelers have developed two new itinerant occupational specialties: peddling linoleum rugs from door to door and spray-painting barns and houses. The latter originally consisted only of spraying the metal parts of buildings with aluminum paint, although today Travelers are beginning to paint the wooden parts of buildings as well. Both of these specialties are not really new, however, but grew out of a need for summer employment in the mule trading days. Mule trading was a seasonal occupation lasting from the middle of September to the end of April. When the season was over, Travelers took their families to one of the Southern stock centers to camp for the summer. About the time of the appearance of automobiles and trucks, the men began to go out into the countryside near to where they were camped to peddle and paint. As the mule trade breathed its last, many traders found it necessary to adopt as fulltime employment what was once only a summer diversion from the normal routine of the mule trading way of life.

Today painting and peddling have no season as such, although Travelers tell me there is less to do in winter generally because of inclement weather. As in the mule trading days, the men in their new occupations often form partnerships and share their profits, though this is much more common for painters than for peddlers. During the part of the year the children are in school, the men go into the countryside with pickup trucks and ply their trades. Sometimes the men will be gone as long as a month or more at a time, although some return to their homes and families every weekend. During the summer months the men often take their families with them, and painters go as far north and west as Michigan and Minnesota. Painters say business is better "up country" where the farm buildings are bigger, and they can get a better price for painting them. Rug peddlers, on the other hand, tend to restrict their travels primarily to the southern states of Georgia, North Carolina, South Carolina, Mississippi, Alabama, and Kentucky, where they can still find unpainted shacks along unpaved country roads. "Up country," peddlers say, "people don't use linoleum rugs no more."

Today the Travelers are a rapidly changing people. They are losing the old ways and are taking up new. Perhaps the two greatest forces for change are education and an increasingly intimate contact with middle class American values through such sources as the mass media. Also, occupations such as mule trading, painting, and linoleum peddling are dying out so that most Travelers feel that these occupations will soon be gone. Some Travelers are finding other things to do. In their own community, for example, there are two stores owned and operated by Travelers. Another Traveler works for a fuel oil company, while others have driven cookie and milk trucks, and every day more Travelers make similar outside contacts.

Education is one of the most potent forces in changing Irish Traveler society. There are probably more Irish Travelers in school today than at any other time in Traveler history. Furthermore, a few high school age boys even aspire to attend college.

The greatest barrier now remaining between the Travelers and the outside world is their "Travelerness," for lack of a better term. Although all Travelers consider themselves good Americans, none wants to be cut off from the security and sense of community that his village or group has to offer. Parents who want their boys to attend college want them to go no farther than the local community college, for to go farther would separate them from the warmth and security of their people. Parents are very much afraid that their children will fall under the bad influences of hippies, marijuana, and wild women. Summing it up, one Traveler woman said, "At home they have the best of everything. They want the opportunities of . . . the Village. They don't want to take a chance."

### IRISH TRAVELER CANT

So far my research on the Irish Travelers has been primarily linguistic (Harper and Hudson 1971). While conducting field work among the Travelers, I discovered that this group still retains an argot, a mode of disguised linguistic communication which they call "the Cant." I first learned of the existence of Cant when some Traveler children plied me with the question: "Hey Mister! Do you know the Cant?" and then proceeded to spout a list of strange words, an episode that would be repeated, perhaps, a dozen times while I was in the field.

Cant uses the phonology and morphology of the host dialect of English and is not a language in the conventional sense, but a jargon akin to pig-Latin. In fact, the Travelers themselves regard it in this light. As one Traveler stated:

> Cant . . . it's more of a damned dog-Latin than anything else. It originated right out of the original Irish language. Of course, there's none of us that can really talk that—the Irish Brogue. Of course, we might have sometimes a touch of it, more or less, but that's as far as we can go. But we can't talk the real brogue, so we just pick up what they call Cant.

Traveler children confuse Cant with pig-Latin and are often hard pressed to differentiate the two, indicating again that in the Traveler way of thinking they are not radically different. As a nine-year-old Traveler boy stated, "Cant and pig-Latin are sort of the same."

The difference between the two, basically, is that pig-Latin is a systematic modification of English for the purpose of disguising meaning from those who do not understand the modifications. Cant on the other hand, although it began as a systematic modification of Irish Gaelic, has now become frozen into a set of variant words. Thus the Cant speaker can simply plug these words into an English sentence, as is necessary, to disguise meaning from non-Travelers.

Cant, therefore, is a secret mode of communication, and this secrecy is of primary importance to understanding its function (Harper and Hudson n.d.). Traditionally, Cant was passed from generation to generation serving to isolate the Travelers from non-Travelers economically and socially. One Traveler said, "The word 'Cant,' to us, means you can't understand us." This emphasis upon secrecy was further expressed in statements made by other Traveler informants when asked to give examples of Cant.

Originally, according to informants, Cant was used by the Travelers to communicate with each other in their business dealings. In fact, when the Travelers were asked how they use it they replied, "Oh, it was a talk we used in tradin' but we don't use it much any more." However, a semantic analysis of sentences and phrases of Traveler origin indicates a much wider and more important usage for Cant than the purely economic one suggested in the Traveler statement. Out of the approximately two-hundred fifty sentences and phrases I collected, no more than twenty deal specifically with the mule and horse trade or any other common Traveler occupations, while over one-hundred and twenty, or nearly half, are in the nature of warnings and commands. This suggests that Cant also has the function of aiding the Travelers in situations of danger, stress, or adversity coming from outside their community. This distinction between the two functions of Cant, however, may be one the Travelers themselves do not make. It is probable, in fact, that in the Traveler way of thinking, the two functions are inseparably intertwined in that the second function developed as a result of the first.

To understand what I mean, you have to understand the manner in which the Travelers conduct their business affairs. Traveler business practices are reminiscent of the kind of barter economics practiced by our American forebears and are similar to those of practically any traveling salesman or used car salesman today. Their objective is to make the best deal possible. In other words, in an economic system with a sliding price scale, to stay in business it is sometimes necessary to take a loss which is made up on subsequent sales. However, as in all such shrewd business dealings, the customer sometimes feels, after it is all over, that he has been cheated, whether it is necessarily true or not. In his anger, he may seek some sort of recourse by finding and confronting the person who sold him the merchandise. Yet, the salesman, having realized a profit, will not want to lose it. Thus, it is in connection with such confrontations that Cant is most effectively used by the Travelers. In other words, Cant is not used to cheat people but is simply used to maintain the economic advantage in business dealings.

To illustrate one of these situations, imagine an angry farmer approaching within earshot of an Irish Traveler encampment. He feels cheated in a mule trade and wants his mule and money back. Upon noticing the farmer's approach and wanting to retain possession of the mule and whatever he got to boot (that is, money or barter beyond an even swap), the trader tells his partner, "Put the *mayler* (mule) in the *kul* (swamp), the *gyuk* (man) is *thawriyin araysh* (coming back)."[2] When the farmer reaches the camp, the trader tells him that the mule has been traded off. He then makes every effort to placate the farmer and to convince him that the trade has not been such a bad one after all and that the farmer should go home and forget the whole thing.

Rarely, the situation would arise where the farmer was not to be satisfied with anything short of the trader's arrest. In such a case, Cant served as a warning device. When a Traveler saw the farmer approaching with the sheriff in tow, he would say to the trader, "*misliy* (go) the *sheyjog* (sheriff) is comin'" or "I saw the *sheyjog* (sheriff) up there an' he is *thawriyin* out (swearing out a warrant) an' he's gona *sawlk* your *jiyl* (take you away)." Thus, if the farmer or sheriff or anyone else were within hearing distance, they would not understand what the Travelers were saying, and the trader could get away unscathed.

Finally, Cant has one more important function, that of identifying its speakers as members of a particular group. Thus when the boys asked, "Hey Mister! Do you know the Cant?" they in effect were inquiring "Are you one of us—are you a Traveler?" In fact, the Travelers themselves have described to me situations where Cant was used to identify fellow Travelers.

In summary, Cant is a secret argot brought to America by Irish itinerants during the Irish Potato Famine. In the Old Country it was known as Shelta and was used by Irish itinerants in their business dealings and as a warning device in much the same manner Cant is used by the Irish Travelers today. There are indications, however, that Cant is being used much less now than in the past. While Travelers thirty-five years of age or older may know from one hundred to one hundred and fifty words, the younger generation retains fewer than seventy-five words. And there are indications that the number of Cant words retained will grow fewer as the years go by. The Travelers state that non-Travelers are suspicious of people who talk differently and that keeping secrets really is not the proper thing to do. Also, the priest discourages the use of Cant as one of those old customs the Travelers ought to forget.

## CONCLUSION

As evidenced by my data on the Irish Travelers, Southern gypsy research is a fertile field of investigation, and is one that has barely been researched. Yet, at the same time I indicated that the Irish Travelers are undergoing rapid changes. Future changes will probably occur in the form of out-marriage, the loss of their uxorilocal residence pattern and the loss of their Cant, all of which will have very definite negative effects in terms of Traveler group cohesiveness and identity. This is especially true when combined with the other factors previously mentioned—education and increasing contact with middle class American society. Referring to the Traveler way of life and to past and future changes one Traveler said, "It's coming when they will have to get off the road. The road is expensive with all the motel bills and gas and other things. They don't make buildings with metal roofs anymore. The rug business is going out too, going to tile and hardwood floors. In ten years it will be gone unless they find something else to do."

My limited information tells me that the other Gypsy groups in the South are undergoing similar rapid changes. No doubt much of their traditional way of life will be lost in the next decade. The burden of recording these life ways before they are gone will rest upon the shoulders of the anthropologist, whose field techniques are uniquely suited to the research demands of gypsy studies.

In conclusion, I would like to raise several basic questions, each of which would be a good beginning point for further research: (1) Are there more than four gypsy groups in the South, and how are they related to one another? (2) Do the Romany Gypsy groups still retain and use the Romany Language; and how do they use it? (3) Exactly what part did the Romany Gypsy groups play in the history of the rural South? (4) How do traveling peoples such as the gypsies appraise the personalities of prospective customers in order to gain the advantage over them? (5) Exactly how many "gypsies" are there in the South? Undoubtedly there are many other questions that might be raised concerning the Southern gypsy groups, but it is by now obvious that here lies a fertile area of anthropological research in the South.

## NOTES

1. My field work began in January of 1968, continuing with several interruptions until June of that year. Subsequently I returned for short visits and a ten-day period of field work in August, 1969. I plan to do additional field work and research on the Irish Travelers in the future.

2. Unfortunately it has not been possible to indicate the correct phonetic values for Cant words. The interested reader should refer to Harper and Hudson (1971).

## REFERENCES

Boles, Don and Jacqueline Boles, 1959. The Gypsies' Doctor in Georgia. *Journal of the Gypsy Lore Society* 38:55-62.

Bonos, Arlene Helen, 1942. Roumany Rye of Philadelphia. *American Anthropologist* 44:257-75.

Çoker, Gülbün, 1966. Romany Rye in Philadelphia: A Sequel. *Southwestern Journal of Anthropology* 22:85-100.

Greene, Patrick, 1933-34. Some Notes on Tinkers and Their "Cant." *Béaloïdeas, the Journal of the Folklore of Ireland Society* 4:259-63.

Harper, Jared, 1968. Tinker Cant in the South. Current Research Report presented at the 67th annual meeting of the American Anthropological Association, Seattle, Washington.

————, 1969a. Irish Itinerants in the South. A paper presented at the 68th annual meeting of the American Anthropological Association, New Orleans, La.

————, 1969b. Irish Traveler Cant: An Historical, Structural, and Sociolinguistic Study of an Argot. A master's thesis, University of Georgia, Athens, Georgia.

Harper, Jared and Charles Hudson, 1971. Irish Traveler Cant. *Journal of English Linguistics*, in press.

————, n.d. Irish Traveler Cant in its Social Setting. Manuscript.

Muller, Edwin, 1941. Roving the South with the Irish Horse Traders. *Reader's Digest* (July, 1941), 59-63.

Ryan, George, 1967. The Irish Travelers. *Ave Maria* (March 18, 1967), 16-18.

# The Impact of Coal Mining on the Traditional Mountain Subculture

EDWARD E. KNIPE and HELEN M. LEWIS

THIS paper developed from a recent study of the effects of mechanization on coal miners and their families in the Southwest triangle of Virginia[1] (Lewis and Knipe 1969). In order to determine the impact of mechanization upon underground work organization and the social life of miners and their wives, nine mines, representing the major coal-getting technologies were sampled. The data for the study came from underground observations in each mine, taped interviews with each miner, and semi-structured interviews with each wife.

We had assumed that coal miners and their families, because of the nature of coal mining itself, would exhibit patterns of behavior and thoughts which differed from the older mountain patterns. We found, however, many parallels between our sample responses and what has been written about traditional Appalachian culture. We became interested in distinguishing traditional mountain ways and the effects of coal mining. Since our sample lived in the same region as the traditional highlander, it would be an easy matter to dismiss these similarities between miners' responses and traditional mountain values as nothing more than the "perpetuation of the mores" or simple diffusion.

Rather, we will try to show how and what structural changes occurred in this particular area of Appalachia as a result of coal mining and what resulted from these changes. It is our contention that coal mining reinforced and helped preserve certain traditional mountain ways while at the same time it changed other relationships. It is a fundamental point of this paper that coal mining created a system of "peasant-like" structures over the traditional Appalachian culture. We will also attempt to show how changes in coal mining with the introduction of modern technological processes have been responsible for the transformation of these peasant-like characteristics into what might be called urban patterns, thus resulting in peasantry being lost.

Southern Appalachia cannot be thought of as a unified region having a homogeneous culture (Campbell 1921; Vance 1960). However most studies of isolated communities or counties in the Southern Appalachians find very similar orientations and characteristics of the inhabitants. Ford's "Passing of Provincialism" (1962), Pearsall's *Little Smoky Ridge* (1959), Brown's *Beech Creek Studies* (1950; 1952), Weller's *Yesterday's People* (1965), and Stephenson's *Shiloh* (1968) find quite similar orientations of persons living in the area. Among these orientations are: traditionalism, individualism, fatalism, and a present-orientation. Howard K. Beers (1946) felt that the general isolation of mountain people and their strong kinship affiliations and orientations placed them into a "folk-like" category. Cressy (1949) spoke of the area as an "arrested frontier culture" having many characteristics of a folk culture but lacking the stability and class stratification of a peasant culture.

That part of the Appalachians with which we are concerned is the portion of the Alleghany-Cumberland mountains in which bituminous coal mining developed. Portions of southwest Virginia, eastern Kentucky and southern West Virginia form this area. It is an area which was the most isolated portion of the Southern Appalachians and which developed and maintained for a longer period of time those patterns referred to as "traditional mountain culture."

The area had a relatively long period of virtual isolation in the nineteenth century. Up until the Revolution it was an area to pass through or skirt around, since it was covered by extensive forests, the soil was poor, and there was little level land. Those seeking good farmland went farther into the Blue Grass, the Tennessee Valley, or farther north (Lewis 1968).

Since the bottom lands near the rivers and streams provided the only acreage suitable for agricultural use, original settlements followed "line" patterns. With population increase the settlers moved farther up the hillsides and hollows, usually along kin lines so that one finds even today valleys and hollows named after and resided in by extended kin. Moving away from the arable river bottoms meant moving onto lands less suitable for traditional agricultural practices. Without knowledge of terracing and crop rotation the land soon became barren and subject to erosion and flooding. The indiscriminate cutting of lumber and general exploitation led to devastation of the natural environment. It is not difficult to explain the fatalistic orientation attributed to the Southern Highlander. The inability to predict the future because of complete dependence upon the environment presents one with little alternative but to be present-oriented. Within a subsistence economy there is little need for a complex system of social organization. With limited contact with the outside world there are few from whom one can "borrow" practices or beliefs; therefore tradition can be the only source for present practices. Because of this traditional and kin orientation, the placing of outsiders into meaningful social categories is useless. Given the level of technology of the original settlers and the nature of the environment, these orientations "fit" the situation.

### THE COAL MINING CULTURE: A CASE OF PEASANTRY GAINED

Ford (1965) draws a parallel between the values of rural Appalachia and those of a Mexican peasant society, attributing similarities to the conditions of poverty which exist in the Mexican village of Azteca and in communities of eastern Kentucky. Although isolated rural mountain people and Mexican peasants may share certain values, we suggest that something more than poverty link the two together and this something did not appear in Appalachia until after the introduction of coal mining. According to Eric Wolf (1955) the criteria by which a society is defined as peasant are *both* economic and socio-political. The peasant society is defined through its relationship to the larger urban society, and only when there is subjugation to the larger society is one able to state that a condition of peasantry exists (Foster 1967). Some of the same values existed in the isolated mountain area where living was meager, but the structure which produces peasantry was not present until coal mining.

Looking specifically at southwest Virginia, we find that the first load of coal was shipped from Wise County in 1892. With the introduction of mining, mining camps were built near the mines, up the hollows, some being more isolated than the original farming settlements. Instead of following the stream beds like the residence patterns of the original settlers, the camps were built along the railroad tracks leading to the mine tipple.

The fertile bottom land where the best farms had been located were often the only land suitable for the erection of mine offices and houses. The former independent landowners either sold at a profit and retired or parted with their land and became day laborers. The wage system replaced barter and exchange. The commissary or company

store substituted imported food and store goods for household manu-
factures of the past. Roads were poor or non-existant. Some mountain
men were attracted to the coal mines. Hillside farming produced a
meager, difficult existence, and the wages, the goods, the houses,
and the pleasures of the mining camps were attractive. Others were
forced into mining by fraudulent land sales and soil depletion.

The coming of the coal industry did not open the mountains to the
mainstream of modern society. The markets, ownership, and control
of the coal operations were in Pittsburgh, New York, and the industrial centers of the East and Midwest. While the coal moved out to
supply the industrial centers of the country, the miners became more
isolated and less able to move because of the elaborate system of paying
in scrip and forced patronage of the company stores which kept the
miner in "debt peonage."

In addition to the physical isolation and the dependency of the
miner upon the coal companies, there developed a stratification system
which made the miner socially isolated. Mining brought in social
class distinctions unknown to the mountain culture. Trading centers
and residential towns were developed for the managers, chemists, engineers, geologists, and other personnel brought in to provide professional services to the mining companies. These towns and villages
were not large, most of them around 2,000 population, but they were
connected with the outside world. Surrounded by mountain settlements and mining camps, they were middle class islands, bringing
"civilization" from the outside world to the crude and harsh life of
mountain farming and coal mining. Like colonists in a foreign land,
the owner-operators and their wives developed country clubs, ladies
literary clubs, and Episcopal and other "establishment" churches
which contrasted with the informal sectarian religion or the un-
classified "company church" of the coal camp.

Although some may object to our use of the term peasantry or
peasant-like to describe the situation of the early coal miner in the
region, we feel that Firth's extension of peasantry to non-agricul-
turists has merit, especially when one defines as peasantry those
situations characterized by certain structural relationships to a larger
society (1952). For example, the central theme of Foster's approach is
that those in peasantry have very little control over the conditions
which govern their lives (1967). Looking at the traditional Appalachian,
we note that very few if any of his ties were to social units outside
the immediate geographical area in which he resided. Although the
traditional highlander was subject to the rigors of his environments—
poor land, primitive technology—he was nevertheless somewhat in-

dependent. Once he moved into the coal camps, however, the only decision he made was to stay or to leave. While in the camp he had no choice over the house in which he would live, the place in which he would work, where he would buy his groceries and other commodities, or how much he would be paid. In other words there were no alternatives. Decisions about his life were made by others. If he went to church, that church was provided by the company. If he or his children were sick, he went to the company doctor or to no doctor at all. The doctor's pay, the pay of the man who checked the cars of coal he loaded during the day, the cost of dynamite, and the cost of carbide used in his lamp were all deducted from his wages. In early coal camps there were no unions, and companies were often very lax in maintaining safety conditions. If the miner felt that conditions were unsafe underground, he had no recourse other than to quit. If the company docked his pay because he loaded too much slate, he had no appeal. The money he received for his wages were subject to markets at the national level and to the caprice of the local managers. While the traditional highlander could decide not to work one day, the coal miner could not. If he did not show up for work, he might find himself and his family moved out of the company house.

Those mountain men who remained on their subsistence farms and worked sporadically in the mines were more independent. They were not, however, considered desirable workers by owners and operators (Verhoeff 1911).

Foster points out that the peasant is poor. Although the traditional mountain family had a meager subsistence, they were not economically dependent. There were few economic differences among members of the population. Poverty, as we perceive it, is relative rather than absolute. Persons brought in with the coal industry—owners, managers, professional people—enjoyed a level of living higher than the Appalachian who left his farm to work in the mines and live in the coal camps. Without some type of standard the highlander did not know he was poor.

Foster presents the idea that peasant leadership is weak or nonexistent because "the more powerful extra-village leaders who hold vested interests in peasant communities cannot afford to let local leaders rise, since they would constitute a threat to their control" 1967:8). It has been suggested that the low standards of education provided by coal companies, the resistance by the coal companies to pay any local school taxes, and the system of debt peonage maintained by the use of scrip and the later "unlimited credit" were effective means of preventing the emergence of local leaders. What strong leadership did emerge was through the unions, which developed later and on the national level.

Foster says that the powerlessness inherent in peasantry leads to a search for structures which will permit a maximizing of limited opportunities. Two such patterns are suggested—the patron-client relationship and fictive kinship. In the patron-client relationship the peasant seeks out those who are links to the outside, those associated with or attached to the "Great Tradition" (1967:9). Accounts of the early coal camps picture owners and operators as either highly exploitative of their labor or very paternalistic (Ross 1933; Lantz 1958; Caudill 1962). The paternalistic owner-operator was one who looked after his people and who was concerned with the welfare of each miner and his family and who, in turn, received the undivided loyalty of his workers. In some of the small mines in our study we found owners who assumed a very paternalistic attitude toward their miners. They paid them whenever they needed money, extended loans, co-signed notes, and took a great deal of interest in the welfare of the miner's family.

Some of the intense hostilities and bitter conflicts which developed in the unionization process in the area can be seen from this "personalistic" attachment the miner had to the operators and the later feeling that his personal loyalties had been betrayed. Personal behavior can be violent as well as friendly. Mining resulted in the development of strong peer-groups of miners with strong identification and loyalties, which may be considered as substitute kin groups and support structures in the face of this powerlessness.

The introduction of mining also affected non-miners in the region. Those who attempted to maintain traditional rural patterns of agriculture were in many cases forced off the land, and the poorly educated sons of rural people were lured into mining.

Some of the characteristics of traditional mountain culture were encouraged and maintained by coal mining, fitting in well with peasant-like dependency or maintained by the social and physical isolation of mining. Suspicion of outsiders was reinforced after the traditional highlander had been exploited by large coal interests. The individualism of the mountaineer, which has been described not in terms of independence but as avoidance of social responsibilities, was also encouraged by the paternalism of the coal camps (Weller 1965). There was some breakdown of the extended family due to the mobility of families within the coal fields, but loyalties shifted to the worker peer-groups and did not extend relationships to heterogeneous outside groups.

Handloading, the simplest and earliest technology of coal mining, helped maintain some of the mountain man's individualism. In the handloading mine each man works his own "place." He is isolated from his fellow workers and generally sees the foreman or other miners only once or twice a day. Goodrich (1925) calls this isolation the "miner's freedom" and maintains that the miner was a free agent underground. Our data from handloading miners showed they preferred to work alone rather than with a "buddy." Owners of some of the handloading mines complained that many miners would set a quota for the day and when this quota was completed they left. Some operators of these small handloading operations tried to win the loyalty of their men through "old fashioned" paternalism or by such economic controls as money lending or the operation of small credit groceries.

## Changes in Mining: Peasantry Lost

Changes in mining technology increased the productivity of the miner and resulted in widespread unemployment in the coal fields. With the introduction of conventional mining techniques in the 1920s and continuous mining after World War II, the productivity rose from 4.47 tons per man day to 17 tons per man day in 1964. The number of miners decreased from 704,793 in 1923 to 131,752 in 1966 (National Coal 1964; 1968).

The changes in mining technology also resulted in changes in worker organization. Unlike handloading methods of mining, in both conventional and continuous sections men work together as teams. The exact relationships between miners in these two technologies would differ, but the fact that a machine is operated by two or more men and has to be supported continually through contact with other miners brings the miner into very close relationship with others (Knipe 1967). In conventional and continuous mines there is no self-determination of work pace. This is either established by the work group or by the design of the machine. Another result of this working together is the increased bond of solidarity for safety reasons. Coal mining is the most dangerous occupation in the United States. It has the highest fatality and accident rate as compared with any other occupation or industry. With an increasing division of labor as a result of changing technology, men became increasingly dependent on others. The men who bolt the roof or set safety timbers have to be trusted to do their job. The man operating a machine has to be felt competent enough to control that machine so as not to hurt others working nearby. This interdependency is reflected in the question concerning working alone or with others. Only 14 per cent of the conventional miners said they would rather work alone, while 9 per cent of the continuous miners felt this way (Lewis and Knipe 1969).

Probably the most significant consequence of changes in technology was the trend toward increasing stability in employment. The market was leveled somewhat with the loss of the home consumer of coal and the increasing demands for coal as a fuel in generating electrical power. Because of this, mines and mining companies could predict future needs, thereby guaranteeing to the miner future employment. The mechanization of mining increased predictability underground as well. The mining of coal became a more rational process in which the machine created regularity in mining procedures.

Along with these changes in technology, other changes in community patterns occurred (Lewis 1967). After 1940 the companies began selling the company-owned houses to the individual miners and the stores to outside businessmen. There were several reasons for selling the houses: the companies found the houses expensive to keep up, and making the miner a property owner and taxpayer relieved the operator of the obligations for repairing, installing, and maintaining roads, water supplies, sewage and garbage disposal facilities, and other public facilities. The building of roads and the ownership of automobiles by the workers reduced the necessity for housing close to the mines.

These changes were not without their problems. Residents reported the great "panic" of the housewife when announcements were made that the company store would be closed (Evanoff 1960). Some of the coal camps were completely demolished by the companies, others became smaller home-owning communities made up of working and retired miners, and some changed into dilapidated rural slums.

Accompanying the changes in mining and mining communities was the development of several types of occupational family types in the area (Lewis 1970). One is the unionized, skilled mechanized miner who works in the larger mining operation. This miner and his family with the independence of stable employment at relatively high wages and union contract have approached the more urban patterns of living.

Another type is the "independent" handloader who works in the small, marginal truck mines and shifts from job to job. His work is intermittent due to his own work patterns and the shifting nature of small marginal truck mines in which capital investment is low and movement is frequent. Although he gives the appearance of operating like the old independent mountain man, the independent handloader no longer has his subsistence farm to return to; thus he is more tied to the job for survival. His work patterns may be interpreted not as a sign of independence, but as a form of sabotage to express his frustrations, or it may be an expression of his lack of commitment to "getting ahead" so that he works only enough to maintain his meager but acceptable standard of living. We found the handloaders less likely to own their homes and maintain family gardens than the stable, mechanized miner (Lewis and Knipe 1969).

Intermediate between these two types is the non-unionized miner who works in small mechanized truck mines. These mines work less productive seams of coal leased from larger companies. The whole operation is dependent upon the larger mines and moves frequently due to leasing arrangements or physical conditions. The miner's lack of education and his ties to his kin still hold him to the area and to coal mining because it is the only job available. Although Cressey (1953) suggested that coal mining resulted in the loss of ties to extended kin, we found that the coal mining families of the area belong to large kin groups, and they live and interact in a world of kin (Lewis 1970). It seems likely that differential migration from the coal fields has occurred so that those with less education and larger kin groups have remained in the area. Those who had moved into the area from outside to enter mining, thus breaking their ties with extended kin, were probably more mobile and left the area when mechanization resulted in large scale unemployment. This is obvious in the case of Negro and foreign born miners who migrated out. In some ways the kin ties may hold the miner to the area and to the job, but in other ways it also frees him from complete dependence upon the job, for he has the resources of his extended kin groups to give him assistance in times of unemployment.

### EMERGENCE OF URBAN PATTERNS

One indication of the change to more urban values and patterns of interaction by those employed in the stable mechanized mines are the differential attitudes which indicate fatalism on the part of the miner and his family. We mentioned earlier that one of the values of the rural mountain subculture and of peasantry was fatalism: man has no control over his environment; he is subjugated to environmental forces or supernatural will, unable to control his destiny; death, illness, and accidents occur when it is "your time," and there is nothing you can do about it.

In opposition to this, the value orientation of urban middle class America defines a person's position as one of directing life; nature is something to be controlled, God works through man, and man is charged with the responsibility of changing his condition and controlling the world about him.

In reply to questions concerning control over life, satisfaction with life as it is, and ability to plan for oneself or one's children, those mining families who had had a longer period of steady employment at relatively higher wages and had enjoyed a higher standard of living for a longer period of time were less fatalistic. While 93 per cent of the handloaders' wives felt that man should be satisfied with his condition, only 43 per cent of those stably employed in mechanized mines expressed these views. Intermediate types of truck miners whose employment had been less stable were in between. Age did not affect this; both young and old in unstable situations were fatalistic (Lewis and Knipe 1969).

In terms of ambitions and plans for children, handloaders' wives were much less optimistic about being able to encourage their children to remain in school. While 75 per cent of the mechanized miners' wives felt that they would have some success in encouraging their children to finish school, only 45 per cent of the handloaders' wives felt they could plan or help their children in this way.

The mechanized miners were no longer dependent on company stores and small credit groceries, and they were able to budget, save, and pay cash for groceries. The truck miners' wives continued to be dependent on the credit grocer, who was an important resource in times of unemployment. They could not afford the luxury of giving up these informal networks of obligations and responsibilities which the ties to the small market represented.

The increase in community participation—ties to the greater society —also reflected these differences. The economically secure were the highest participators in church activities, politics, and community organizations. Fifty per cent of the wives of mechanized miners participated in clubs or organizations as compared to 18 per cent of the truck miners' wives. Seventy-nine per cent of the mechanized miners voted as compared to 36 per cent of the handloaders.

### CONCLUSIONS

We have illustrated some of the changes associated with the introduction of coal mining in one part of the Southern Appalachians. We have suggested that these changes account for or explain the various social types found in this area. In doing so, the concept of "peasantry" has been used to identify some of the main structural dimensions associated with these types. We have suggested that the stably employed mechanized miners have moved toward urbanized values and social organization, while the truck miners, both handloaders and mechanized miners, represent various degrees of peasantry.

Although some may feel that we have extended the concept of peasantry far beyond its usual reference to agricultural peoples, we feel that such usage is justifiable if one is to become sensitized to those underlying structural dimensions which have explanatory value. To label a social configuration as peasant does not explain it; to restrict the usage of the term gives it little analytical value. If, as Foster suggests, peasantry is characterized by dependency, powerlessness, and lack of autonomy then we can apply it to a wide variety of social phenomena. This study illustrates such an application.

## NOTES

1. A somewhat longer version of this paper was read at the 1969 meeting of the Southern Anthropological Society, New Orleans, Louisiana, March 14, 1969.

This study was made possible through two grants from the U. S. Bureau of Mines: Grant EA-7, "A Pilot Study of Methods to Determine the Impact of Changes in Mining Technology on the Attitudes, Behavior, and Productivity of Bituminous Coal Miners" and Grant EA-12, "A Pilot Study of Techniques to Analyze Data on the Impact of Changes in Mining Technology on the Attitudes, Behavior and Productivity of Bituminous Coal Miners." The research was carried out between June 1, 1967 and August 31, 1968.

## REFERENCES

Beers, Howard W., 1964. Highland Society in Transition. *Mountain Life and Work*, (Spring), pp. 1-27.

Brown, James S., 1952. The Family Group in a Kentucky Mountain Farm Community and The Farm Family in a Kentucky Mountain Neighborhood. Kentucky Agricultural Experimental Station Bulletins, 587-588.

———————— 1962. *Eastern Kentucky Resources Development Project* (Lexington: University of Kentucky Press).

Caudill, Harry, 1962. *Night Comes to the Cumberlands* (Boston: Little, Brown and Co.).

Campbell, John C., 1921. *The Southern Highlander and His Homeland* (New York: Russell Sage Foundation).

Cressey, Paul F., 1953. Social Disorganization and Reorganization in Harlan County, Kentucky. In *Sociology: A Book of Readings*, Samuel Koenig, et al., eds. (New York: Prentice Hall), pp. 576-582.

Evanoff, Vonda Sue, 1960. Dunham, Kentucky. Community Studies. Library, Clinch Valley College, Wise, Virginia.

Ford, Thomas R., 1962. The Passing of Provincialism. In *The Southern*

*Appalachian Region*, Thomas R. Ford, ed. (Lexington: University of Kentucky Press), pp. 9-34.

--------------------, 1965. The Effects of Prevailing Values and Beliefs on the Perception of Poverty in Rural Areas. In *Problems of Chronically Depressed Rural Areas* (North Carolina State University: Agricultural Policy Institute), pp. 33-43.

Foster, George M., 1967. What is a Peasant? in *Peasant Society: A Reader*, Jack M. Potter, May N. Diaz and George M. Foster, eds. (Boston: Little, Brown and Co.), pp. 2-14.

Firth, Raymond, 1963. *Elements of Social Organizations* (Boston: Beacon Press).

Goodrich, Carter, 1925. *The Miner's Freedom: A Study of the Working Life in Changing Industry* (Boston: Marshall Jones Company).

Knipe, Edward E., 1967. Changes in Mining and Worker Interaction. Paper presented at the International Seminar on Social Change in the Mining Community, Part I, Jackson Mill, West Virginia.

Knipe, Edward E. and Helen M. Lewis, 1969. Toward a Methodology of Studying Coal Miner's Attitudes. PB 184665, U. S. Dept. of Commerce, Springfield, Virginia.

Lantz, Herman R., 1958. *People of Coal Town* (New York: Columbia University Press).

Lewis, Helen M., 1967. The Changing Communities in the Southern Appalachian Coal Fields. Paper presented at the International Seminar on Social Change in Mining Community, Part I, Jackson Mill, West Virginia.

--------------------, 1968. Subcultures of the Southern Appalachians. *The Virginia Geographer* 3:2-8.

--------------------, 1970. Occupational Roles and Family Roles: A Study of Coal Mining Families in the Southern Appalachians. Ph.D. dissertation, University of Kentucky.

Lewis, Helen M. and Edward E. Knipe, 1969. The Sociological Impact of Mechanization on Coal Miners and Their Families. *Proceedings of the Council of Economics*, American Institute of Mining, Metallurgical, and Petroleum Engineers, 268-307. And PB 183849, U. S. Dept. of Commerce, Springfield, Virginia.

National Coal Association, 1964. *Bituminous Coal Data* (Washington, D. C.: National Coal Association).

--------------------, 1968. *Bituminous Coal Facts* (Washington, D. C.: National Coal Association).

Pearsall, Marion, 1959. *Little Smoky Ridge* (University, Alabama: University of Alabama Press).

--------------------, 1966. Communicating with the Educationally Deprived. *Mountain Life and Work*, (Spring), pp. 3-11.

Ross, Malcolm, 1933. *Machine Age in the Hills* (New York: Macmillan).

Stephenson, John B., 1968. *Shiloh: A Mountain Community* (Lexington, Kentucky: University of Kentucky Press).

Vance, Rupert B., 1960. The Sociological Implication of Southern Regionalism. *The Journal of Southern History* 26:51-52.

Verhoeff, Mary, 1911. *The Kentucky Mountains, Transportation and Commerce, 1750-1911* (Louisville: Filson Club Publication 26).

Weller, Jack, 1965. *Yesterday's People* (Lexington: University of Kentucky Press).

Wolf, Eric R., 1955. Types of Latin American Peasantry: A Preliminary Discussion. *American Anthropologist* 57:452-471.

# The Darlings Creek Peasant Settlements of St. Helena Parish, Louisiana

MILTON B. NEWTON, JR.

IN 1821 the *American Farmer*, a journal devoted to rural life, published "The Peasant and His Wife," which in part ran as follows (Anonymous 1821):

> He: The long, long day again has pass'd
> In sorrow and distress:
> I strive my best—but strive in vain,
> I labor hard—but still remain
> Poor and in wretchedness.

At least since that time, the term "peasant" has not been considered applicable to citizens of the United States. People feel that the term "peasant" is derogatory; avoidance of the term extends, as well, into the ranks of the literati. Reference to standard surveys of peasantry, such as Eric R. Wolf's *Peasants* (1966), shows that the United States is lily-white on distribution maps—in other words, there are no peasants in the United States, or so it would seem. For example, George Foster states categorically, "American farmers, even prior to the introduction of elaborate machinery, were not peasants . . ." (1967:7).

The cultural geographer, E. Estyn Evans, might have had tongue in cheek when he explained: "We may find peasant values persisting among farmers who would resent the term 'peasantry'. . . . The word has always carried an implication of rustic inferiority, and we tend to apply it to countries other than our own" (1956:220). It seems that peasants are what *others* have. Failure to admit that a peasantry exists or existed in the United States makes the many, varied, and excellent studies of peasantry in other places unavailable as theoretical and practical aids in dealing with the complex society of the South.

This is not to say that the peasants of the South have not been studied; indeed, they have been examined many times over. Actually, a number of scholars have touched upon the Southern peasant, but under a variety of names. The historian Owsley, after examining several possible names, settled upon "Plain Folks" (1949), while the agricultural historian Gray subdivided them into poor whites and yeoman farmers (1933). Other historians, such as John Hebron Moore (1958) and Herbert Weaver (1945), have dealt with the people we should call peasants. A few, such as Raper (1936) and Raper and Reid (1941), have spoken specifically of Southern peasants.

A variety of terms have been used to denote the Southern peasant and to connote varying degrees of approval. Most of these are folk terms and can be used only with the greatest care because they are emotionally loaded. The terms include: Hill-Billy (Tennessee), Red-Neck (northern Louisiana), Piney-Woods Folk (wide spread), Sand-Hiller and Clay-Eater (Carolina), Cracker (Georgia and Florida), Cedar-Chopper (central Texas), Congaree (Blue Ridge), Southern Highlander (Appalachia), and many others. With this array, it is not surprising that Owsley chose "Plain Folks" as an over-all term, especially in view of the pejorative quality of many of the other terms.

But the real question at hand is whether any of the people of the South can be classed as peasants. We can, for the moment, accept several leading definitions as valid for their specific purposes and simply use a tabulation of criteria as a check list to judge whether and to what extent some Southerners can be classed as peasants. By this means we may be able to avoid some of the disagreement concerning the traits of peasantry. If the people in question exhibit all or most of the significant traits suggested by each authority, and if these function in the manner implied by the over-all view of peasantry, then we are indeed dealing with a peasantry.

The following table presents the specifically stated positive criteria abstracted from definitions of peasantry by eight authorities. The group includes anthropologists, geographers, and an economist, covering all inhabited continents and spanning publication dates from 1939 through 1967.

Ignoring for the moment pre-peasants (Fallers 1961), post-peasants (Foster 1967:7), sub-peasants (Raper 1936:4), fisher-farmers, hunter-farmers, cuckoo-clock makers, and other folk groups, perhaps we might agree that, based upon this tabulation, a consensus would re-assemble these traits into a functioning whole as follows. A peasant is a member of a rural community of rustic agriculturists, horticulturists, or stockman, who individually or collectively have sufficient

| Tabulation of specifically-stated, positive criteria of peasantry as stated by eight authors. | Redfield (1960:19) | Evans (1956:220-1, 237) | Pfiefer (1956:242ff) | Wolf (1966:2, 8-9, et passim) | Warriner (1939: passim) | Kroeber (1948:248) | Foster (1967:2-13) | Diaz (1967:50-56) |
|---|---|---|---|---|---|---|---|---|
| Agricultural occupation | X | X | X | X | X |  | X | X |
| Part-society, part-culture | X | X |  | X | X | X | X | X |
| Subsistence w/some market | X | X | X | X | X |  | X | X |
| Self-employed/control of land | X | X | X | X | X |  |  | X |
| Customary technology/"conservative" | X | X | X |  | X |  |  | X |
| External controls |  | X | X | X |  |  | X | X |
| Rustic/rural |  | X |  |  | X | X | X |  |
| Man-land bonds | X | X | X |  |  |  |  | X |
| Way of life, not business | X |  | X | X |  |  |  |  |
| Hostility to commercial culture | X |  | X |  |  |  | X |  |
| Market transcends local dealings |  |  |  |  |  | X | X | X |
| Stockmen may be included |  | X | X |  |  |  |  | X |
| Family labor as capital |  | X | X |  |  |  |  |  |
| "Estate"/Bauernstand |  |  | X |  |  |  |  |  |
| Relate to pre-industrial cities |  |  |  |  |  |  | X |  |

control of the land to carry on largely traditional methods of producing mainly customary crops. Such a community supports its labor-supplying households importantly from the land as well as produces certain specific staples demanded by the dominant sections of a larger society and culture in which they participate only partially. The latter partialness stems, on the one hand, from a historic status occupied by the peasant with regard to a historic nobility if the noble shared title to the peasant's land. On the other hand, partialness stems from equally historic relations with the elite of the market town (pre-industrial city) where there originate external economic, political, and religious demands upon the peasant, his community, and his produce. Peasant farming is part of a way of life ("*estate*" or *Bauernstand*) involving a series of historically derived man-land relations which have value in themselves, not merely in their potential for profit. In the partial conflict between these rustic lifeways and the demands and values of the elite of the market town lies the source of hostility toward commercial culture and cities. From the geographical point of view, the peasant community is interesting not only because of its occupying an area of the earth's surface and a segment of the economic network, but also because of its continuing customary manner of altering the landscape and because its simple technology and long tenure point up variation in earth qualities.

## THE DARLINGS CREEK SETTLEMENTS

Turning to a specific group of peasants, the Negroes living along Darlings Creek in northwestern St. Helena Parish, Louisiana, will serve as a convenient example. Though these people are black in a white-dominated society and though they seem to hold certain traits peculiar to themselves, they can serve as samples of a larger, mainly white, Upland South Culture.

Upland South Culture—the Scotch-Irish-and-German frontier—spread in the century from 1750 to 1850 to settle the area from Pennsylvania to central Texas and from southern Illinois to northern Florida (Kniffen and Glassie 1966; Evans 1965 and 1969). It occupied Darlings Creek between 1800 and 1805. The black segment, or caste, in Upland South Culture continues more of traditional practices than does the white group in this region, though there is no clear dichotomy between the cultural forms of blacks and whites, especially in the material and landscape aspects (Newton, 1967). Indeed, black peasants in their relationship with the white elite are quite similar to white peasants in the same relationship. Both also share a single complex of man-land relations which spread and developed from its eighteenth century origin in southern Pennsylvania. Evidence consisting of letters (Anderson Papers n.d.), an unusual farm diary (Lewis n.d.), succession and probate records (St. Helena Parish n.d.), and field investigations reveal not only temporal continuity in the culture of the Upland peasant of St. Helena and continuity between white and black peasants, but also a cultural lag of about one generation between whites and blacks. Historical studies of small farmers support the notion of continuity through time and space for the St. Helena Parish aspect of Upland South (Wailes 1854; Gray 1933:437-82; Moore 1958; Weaver 1945).

At two places along Darlings Creek in the vicinity of Chipola are churches which serve as focal points for two hamlets of black farmers: to the north lies St. Helena Baptist Church; to the south, Pipkin Chapel. Near these two churches are scattered the farmsteads

of the families making up the hamlets which are not mutually ex-
clusive nor completely included within these two church-member-
ships. In each area the leaders in social, economic, and political matters
are often important in the church, though male leaders may not
attend regularly. Leadership tends to cluster around one or two
families and the elders of these families are frequently consulted on
personal and community matters such as new church projects, support
of political candidates, techniques of crop raising, and marketing
arrangements. The eminence of these families is based upon at least
three interrelated considerations: (1) the capacity of the family
leader to deal with the white elite of the parish (county) and the
market; (2) the size and success of the leader's farming enterprise
and of the farms of his close relatives; and (3) the historic status
of that leader as descendant of the founder of a "settlement."

The ability to mediate the demands of parish (county) officials
and to obtain information and favors for one's own is an important
skill, but a demanding role. The status of the leader assures him of
considerate and fairly respectful treatment by both his clients and
his patrons so long as he is successful and so long as the general, regional
sociopolitical situation is stable. The hamlet leader supports the
Police Juror (County Commissioner) of his ward if the parish official obtains favors and concessions for the hamlet leader and his
clients. These channels are built up through a variety of personal
contacts and include the following: (1) There are legal kinship
bonds recognized between white farmers and the white elite, and illegal
kin bonds between blacks and whites. The latter are "recognized" in
many ways, for example, by false deeds of sale in which a white
person conveys land to a black. Blacks speak frankly of their white
kinsmen; whites speak frankly of others' black kinsmen. (2) Faithful
service and participation in an almost proprietary bond is a relation
sometimes overtly expressed as "so-and-so's man." The debt of the
patron is recognized through favors and even deeds of property. (3)
The farmer-leader often permits or arranges rustic favors such as
hunting, fishing, and camping activities for his patron. (4) Preferred-
purchaser-preferred-seller relations often reinforce bonds as in the
case of a parish official of long standing, who owns a produce market.
In addition to being a profitable business, his market represents a
conscious effort at getting all of each of his clients' produce sold.
The skill shown by a hamlet leader in obtaining and maintaining
these and other contacts is one of the determinants of his status.

The success of the leader's farm is at least as important as the size.
In one instance, the hamlet leader farms only about 35 acres, but

quite successfully; he has bought a small tractor, built a new house, and holds the regional record for cotton production per acre. No less important is the need for the leader's close relatives to be successful. To be a big man, one's advice must not only be sought; it also must work.

The historic status of principal descendant of the founder of a settlement is important. The "settlement," in local terminology, is the intermediate level of social integration in a hierarchy including the "homeplace" (family farm), the "settlement" (hamlet), and the "community" (dispersed village).

The settlement is a loose clustering of several peasant family farms, most or all of which belong to kinsmen. It amounts to a dispersed, extended family because it is presided over quite unobtrusively by the eldest male; most of the inhabitants are his sons, brothers, or cousins and their wives and children. Women are nearly the equals of men and, at times, may serve as family heads. Since land is freely salable, non-family members may purchase plots adjacent to or in the midst of the settlement. Settlements are usually named for the principal or founding family, though some are named for the church which includes most of the people in its membership.

While the settlement does not usually have a church at its center, the church is probably the most important single building that is built and maintained by the inhabitants of the settlement. The state of repair of the church is the best single criterion for judging the vigor of the settlement as a social unit. The settlement seems to be the largest entirely peasant unit; it includes no professionals; and it tends to become endogamous. After the third generation, goods and services are exchanged within the settlement with a minimum of money, and such exchanges reinforce social relations.

Several settlements tend to be oriented around a more prosperous settlement, and collectively these are called a community. In or near the community center are located a number of functions missing or infrequent in the settlement. These may include several churches, several cemeteries, a Masonic temple, a post office, scout troops, public schools, retail stores, and service stations.

A community is less populous and more scattered than a town, of which there are two types, both being non-peasant forms belonging to each of the two elites making demands on the peasants. The oldest town in time and function is the courthouse-market town—in this case, Greensburg. Around its courthouse square the main routes of the parish converge, and there too clusters the old elite and its landscape forms: courthouse, newspaper, lawyers' row, county agent's

office, clinic, larger stores, and so forth. Peasants—white or black—
do not live in the courthouse town, and Negroes—peasants or not—
do not live there. Clustering at the edges of the town along the
principal routes are "quarters" of Negroes, some of whom work
in the town and some of whom are even professionals. The courthouse town is a current-day descendant of the pre-industrial city
(Sjoberg 1955).

The second kind of elite center is often the successor to the
courthouse-market town and in many cases has taken on the market
functions and often the court functions of the older type of town.
These more advanced elite centers are the railroad towns, riven apart
by the rails that gave them life. The railroad town with its ware-
houses, double main streets, tracks in the middle of side streets, and
huddles of small factories and poor houses next to the tracks is the
legitimate envoy of "commercial culture" sent into the rural, peasant-
and-courthouse landscape. In the case of St. Helena, there are no
railroads remaining today and, hence, no railroad towns.

## THE USE OF THE LAND

Each family enterprise is a farm ranging from a minimum for
independence of about 25 acres to about 200 acres. However, these
figures can mislead because the areas under cultivation usually vary
between 25 and 35 acres, regardless of total holdings. Furthermore,
the family with only the minimum total acreage must have access
to many additional acres of unimproved land, a continuation of the
ancient commons available for use by all villagers. The uncultivated
woodlands serve as pasture for livestock; as foraging grounds for
gathering firewood, berries, nuts, and herbs; and as hunting and
fishing grounds. For the titular owner, woodlands provide all of
the above as well as new land for use while "resting" other plots
and income from sales of posts, pulpwood, and select hardwoods for
lumber. He may also give part of the woodland to his sons or
sons-in-law, or he may sell it. But so long as it is not under cultivation,
the people of the settlement, especially kinsmen, regard the woods as
open to their uses. (Interestingly at this point, the ward through which
Darlings Creek flows is one of the last to effectively resist closed-
range laws.) As is usually the case with peasants, possession of land
is a primary goal for the individual, but use of that land is participated in by the local group.

The land-use pattern is similar to that followed by some European
peasantry, especially the infield-outfield system of Atlantic Europe.
While there is some shifting of crops in the fields, the more important

aspect is land rotation, a kind of slash-and-burn land management. Any given plot, except those close to the farmstead, may be used for up to 20 years; as it "gets tired," it is abandoned, first to cleared pasture, but gradually returning to forest. As each plot loses productivity and is about to be left idle, similar amounts are cut from the woodland. The clearing is accomplished by deadening trees and burning the slash. Much of the surrounding forest is also burned clear of undergrowth that hinders its use as pasture. Each fall and winter the landscape is dotted with smoke plumes from burning woods.

Fields near the house, as well as the gardens, are seldom taken out of cultivation so long as the farm continues. This is true as well for all of the fields of the smallest farms, for they have no land to rotate. The fertility of these infields is maintained by commercial fertilizer, stockpenning, limited mulching, and burning of grass and stubble before planting.

The Darlings Creek peasant follows a system of crude mixed farming which Wolf might classify as "mesotechnic," or between neotechnic and paleotechnic. Such a classification seems necessary following Wolf's criteria (1966:18-59) and based upon the following traits.

The Darlings Creek farmer spends most of his farming effort on a historic food-and-feed (or subsistence) complex including corn, peas and beans, squash, sweet potatoes, greens, and the raising of pigs. Nearly all of the production of these crops is consumed on the farm as food for man or feed for animals. Cotton, green beans, cucumbers and a few calves are raised for sale.

A customary annual round is followed in which for four months fields lie idle, in the sense that no crops are being grown. However, cattle and mules are penned on the idle fields to forage on the stubble. Pasture grasses are planted only on the most progressive farms or on those specializing as dairies or stock farms, and these would be classed as neotechnic.

The Darlings Creek farmer is aware of basic notions of breeding both plants and animals. He selects seeds following modified folk practices, such as choosing long-kerneled, straight-rowed, large-eared corn for seed. He frequently renews crops with bought seed, choosing varieties that experience or neighbors approve. In the case of commercial crops such as beans, the desires of the commercial buyer are also given weight, largely as a result of instruction by the market owner in Greensburg. The value of improved or hybrid forms is understood, but so is the frequently unprofitable nature of such improvements: yield increases may not be great enough to make acceptance worthwhile. The market must be able to reward the innovation by purchasing the produce, but necessary arrangements do not always exist.

New commercial crops and animals have been accepted in the past and continue to be adopted as profitability becomes apparent. Recall for example, that in their turns corn, sweet potatoes, beans, squash, cotton, bell-peppers, peanuts, and many others were each new crops. New agricultural practices and new machines have also been accepted, including contour plowing, a variety of fertilizers, small tractors, and a host of plow forms. Innovations have been accepted when they have proven useful in terms of local desires, fertility, and access to market. Tradition is important in this as in any other peasant system of tillage; however, it is a realistic traditionalism, willing to accept locally viable innovations.

CONCLUSION

In summary, important data for classifying the Darlings Creek people as "mesotechnic" peasants, following Wolf (1966), are these: 1. They practice permanent cultivation of favored plots (in field-out field). 2. They have a mixed farming ecotype (neotechnic-paleotechnic, or mesotechnic) in which they (a) eat part of their produce; (b) practice seasonal farming and planting ("idle" fields); (c) give some attention to breeding and limited acceptance of hybrids; (d) accept new crops when clearly profitable; and (e) adopt new machinery when clearly profitable and when capital is available. 3. They recognize mercantile domain with both patrimonial and prebendal tendencies. 4. They are organized into extended family clusters of conjugal families changing to nuclear-family units. 5. They practice partible inheritance with some tendency to sell small inheritances to one of a few close relatives. 6. They have many-stranded, dyadic, vertical associations in which both families and family-clusters develop bonds with social, political, and economic superiors, supplemented by many-stranded, polyadic, horizontal associations among co-residents of open country neighborhoods.

As anthropologists would certainly suspect, the significant point is that new tools, crops, and animals have been adapted to the pre-existing system. And since the economic development of the region has been slow, abundant time has been available to integrate these innovations without destroying the peasant character of the culture. Indeed, historical descriptions of the crop complex, garden practices, the system of tillage, the settlement pattern, house and out-building types, and many other traits of the cultural ancestors of Darlings Creek farmers are little changed in their descendants.

Further study of the South as complex society or as a cultural landscape must be aimed, in part, at the question of the role and extensiveness of this peasantry.

## REFERENCES

Anderson [Mollie E.] Papers, n.d. File B-16-1, Archives Room, Louisiana State University Library, Baton Rouge.

Anonymous, 1821. The Peasant and His Wife. *American Farmer* 1:60.

Diaz, May N., 1967. Economic Relations in Peasant Society. In *Peasant Society: A Reader*, Jack M. Potter, May N. Diaz, and George M. Foster, eds. (Boston: Little, Brown, and Co.), pp. 50-56.

Evans, E. Estyn, 1956. The Ecology of Peasant Life in Western Europe. In *Man's Role in Changing the Face of the Earth*, William L. Thomas, Jr., ed. (Chicago: University of Chicago Press), pp. 217-39.

————————, 1965. Cultural Relics of the Ulster-Scots in the Old West of North America. *Ulster Folklife* 11:33-38.

————————, 1969. The Scotch-Irish: Their Cultural Adaptation and Heritage in the American Old West. In *Essays in Scotch-Irish History*, R. R. Green, ed. (London: Routledge & Kegan-Paul), pp. 69-86.

Fallers, L. A., 1961. Are African Cultivators to be Called "Peasants"? *Current Anthropology* 2:108-110.

Foster, George M., 1967. What is a Peasant? In *Peasant Society: A Reader*, Jack M. Potter, May N. Diaz, and George M. Foster, eds. (Boston: Little, Brown, and Co.), pp. 2-14.

Gray, Lewis Cecil, 1933. *History of Agriculture in the Southern United States to 1860* (Washington, D.C.: The Carnegie Institute of Washington).

Kniffen, Fred and Henry Glassie, 1966. Building in Wood in the Eastern United States: A Time-Place Perspective. *The Geographical Review* 56:40-66.

Kroeber, A. L., 1948. *Anthropology* (New York: Harcourt, Brace, and Co.).

Lewis [Jones] Diaries, n.d. Manuscript Farm Diaries, 1910-1962. Microfilm Room, Louisiana State University Library, Baton Rouge.

Moore, John Hebron, 1958. *Agriculture in Ante-bellum Mississippi.* (New York: Bookman Associates).

Newton, Milton B., Jr., 1967. The Peasant Farm of St. Helena Parish, Louisiana: A Cultural Geography. Ph.D. dissertation, Louisiana State University, Baton Rouge.

Owsley, Frank L., 1949. *Plain Folk of the Old South* (Baton Rouge: Louisiana State University Press).

Pfiefer, Gottfried, 1956. The Quality of Peasant Living in Central Europe. In *Man's Role in Changing the Face of the Earth*, William L. Thomas, Jr., ed. (Chicago: University of Chicago Press), pp. 240-77.

Raper, Arthur F., 1936. *Preface to Peasantry: A Tale of Two Black Belt, Counties* (Chapel Hill: University of North Carolina Press).

Raper, Arthur F., and Ira DeA. Reid, 1941. *Share Croppers All* (Chapel Hill: University of North Carolina Press).

Redfield, Robert, 1960. *Peasant Society and Culture* (Chicago: University of Chicago Press).

St. Helena Parish, n.d. Records of the Parish Clerk of Court, Succession and Probate Records, Greensburg, Louisiana.

Sjoberg, Gideon, 1955. The Preindustrial City. *American Journal of Sociology* 60:438-45.

Wailes, Benjamin L. C., 1854. *Report on the Agriculture and Geology of Mississippi* (Jackson: E. Barksdale).

Warriner, Doreen, 1938. *Economics of Peasant Farming* (New York: Oxford University Press).

Weaver, Herbert, 1945. *Mississippi Farmers, 1850-1860* (Nashville: Vanderbilt University Press).

Wolf, Eric R., 1966. *Peasants* (Englewood Cliffs, New Jersey: Prentice Hall, Inc.).

# Living in Urban Milltown

RONALD J. DUNCAN

MILL man makes money. And from this vital essence men were created. Men who could work with their hands and their backs. Men whose minds dimmed with age. Mindless chores. Repeated. Repeated. The loom thumps.

Their minds churned. In the same repetitive acts. The same stories are told when the same group of men gather. The same chores are done every day. The same stories are told every night. It is satisfying to do the same things over and over and over.

Their minds churned. In the same repetitive acts. To come home at night to rock and rock and rock. On the porch, in the living room, in the bedroom. To be more than mindless would be intolerable tomorrow.

Their minds churned. In the same repetitive acts. To come home with no feeling left. A mill is not a place to live. A woman and kids are repetitive acts. A mill town is not a place of love.

Their minds churned. In the same repetitive acts. But, man's mind does not die. On Sunday he is told that he is right. And he needed that. Sometimes man lives by rectitude alone. Calvin is our Savior. To live in grey is not totally colorless.

Their minds churned. In drunkenness. The good Lord gives him a little drink every night. And in the morning he is gone. To the mill? The good Lord? The mill man's world is alone. The little drink. A machine. A bird, maybe a bird.

And the TV roared. And the gas heater mightily conquered the seeping cold. And the seasons passed. And grandmother died. We are not sure where she came from, but we know where she went. And the seasons passed.

## JAKE'S BOTTOMS

Jake's Bottoms is ordered rows of former mill company houses,

49

crazy quiltwork patterns of shotgun shacks, and white cottages with neatly trimmed lawns built on and around a low rolling hill and tied together by being cut off from everything else in the city. Railroad tracks are on one side. A cemetery, a major thoroughfare, the ever looming mill complex, and black neighborhoods complete the isolation. From one crest of the little hill, looking past the corner of the mill one can see the skyline of the city less than a mile away. The gold capitol dome gleams on the sunny days. On the foggy days the 30 story buildings can still be seen in the haze.

But, that is a world that is so far away that no one from Jake's Bottoms ever goes there. Downtown, people get disoriented and lost. It is a foreign and uncomfortable feeling. Nothing good comes from down there, so no one bothers to go. Everything that one could want is within walking distance in Jake's Bottoms. Few people have cars.

Mack's store on the corner has good streak-o-lean bacon and Cokes and just about anything else that one could want. There is a liquor store just down the way. Four generations of family live in the neighborhood, frequently next door to each other, or in the same house. And, no one has to walk more than a block to find a church.

One literally does not have to leave this community of 2,500 souls for anything. Indeed, entering and leaving is rather difficult. Two sides of the community are blocked off, forming a dead-end corner. The streets are narrow and irregular and one-way. One can come to believe that it is impossible to extricate oneself from the maze.

### BILLY JOE

When I was 18, a wife came. At $63.80 a week from the mill I couldn't lose. She came from across the street. She lived with her grandmother. She was sixteen and was unhappy at home. We rented the house next door. Her old man came drunk one night and busted the door. She had a kid the first year we were married. The kid died.

Her brother is pretty good at pool. He and I used to go down in the afternoon, and we'd play till they closed at midnight. He'd hear that some guys had come into town from Moffit, and no matter what he was doin' he'd get up and go down and shoot with them. Sometimes he'd win fifty, maybe hundred dollars a night. He liked tattoos. He had his wife tattooed in the nude on his left arm. Later he had "hell" tattooed there. On his right arm he had tattooed "born to lose."

I've worked off and on at the mill since, I guess, I was 16. My first job was when I was 14. I've worked quite a bit over at Henry's Grocery. He has always been good about taking me back on when I need a job. The only thing about Henry's is that you have to work on Saturday, and you have to work longer every day. At the mill you go at 7:30 and get off at 3:30 if you are on the day shift. But, at the mill you don't ever get to let up. You can't stop what you are doing for a single minute. You don't even get off for lunch. I really don't like working an 8 hour shift without gettin' off at all.

I worked at the mill all summer. Not long ago I quit. I had left the loom, and I stopped just a minute to talk to a guy that I know there. About that time a boss came by. He wasn't even my boss. He asked me what I was doing; I told him. He said that I had been leaving my job too much. He told me to get back to work. Well, I didn't like the way he was talkin'. And, he wasn't even my boss. I told him that he could take his damned job and ram it up where it belonged. And, I left right there on the spot. I didn't even go back to get my check, I just let 'em mail it to me.

I could've gone to one of the big bosses, and they would've straightened things out. But, I didn't like the way the guy was doing. I wasn't goin' to take that, so I just quit.

That Woods family is no account. It's families like that that is makin' our neighborhood go down. This used to be a pretty place to live. The Woods have got a house full of kids, two houses full, and they'd all just as soon kill you as look at you. Kids is runnin' wild. People seem to have lost control.

There are some boys down here that are my age that cause trouble sometimes. They get to drinkin' and get mean. They'll fight a little. My in-laws are like that. It's kinda bad livin' in the same house with them sometimes. They'll start fightin' each other and cussin'. It'll sound like they are tearing the place apart; Lucille will want to do something because its her brothers. I've told her to stay out of it. I don't want to get into that. If she gets her head busted, she'll just have to take whatever happens to her.

I've seen my brother-in-law cuss his own mother to her face. And he lives with her! I'll bet he would hit his own mother. He does a little bootleggin' on the side on the week-ends. He always has beer and wine around. And when they get started drinking, they get mean.

I don't mind drinkin' a beer or two. I used to get drunk. I told the Lord when our first baby died that I'd never touch another drop. And, I didn't for a long time. But, I really got to missin' it. I talked to Mother about it, and she said that the Lord would understand. Sometimes His children make promises that they just cannot live up to.

I really don't think that it is so bad to drink. It is not what goes into a man, but what comes out of him. Take my ol' Dad for instance. He gets drunk every night of the world. But, every morning he gets up and goes to work. And, he is as good as he can be.

He has been that way as long as I have known him. He never does no harm to nobody. He wouldn't hurt a flower. But some people, when they get drunk, they get mean.

My older brother, James, has always had a lot of trouble with his legs. When he was little, he had polio. One of his legs now is no bigger than my arm. But, you hardly ever notice it. He doesn't let people know. When he was in the seventh grade, he had a lot of trouble with his legs. He missed a lot of school that year. And so, he quit. When he got better, he got a job as a roofer. Later on he got me a job with him. Then, I quit school too.

I never was too much on school no way. Why, my Dad never went to school but one day in his life. He didn't like it and ran away. They never did make him go back. He can count and add and figure things as good as anybody. He learned it himself. He educated himself.

I didn't get along too well down at school. I never did like to read too much. Now, I'll read something like the sports in the paper, but nothing like school books. Those teachers always gave me a lot of trouble. They never did like me down there no way. And, I guess you'd say it was mutual. I'd rather a been out playing ball anyhow.

My old man never had much to do with us kids. He was always awfully strict on us. Mother used to try to get him to let us do things, but he never would. He wouldn't let us go out and play with the other kids because he was afraid that we might get hurt. I wanted a bicycle, but he wouldn't buy one because he was afraid something might happen. When I got old enough, I used to go over and spend all my time at my Aunt Chloe's. I'd lived over there if they had let me. But Mother always wanted me to spend time at home. She said it didn't look right. So I'd come home.

When I got old enough, I started spendin' all of my time over at the ball park. When I got off work, I'd go over and play until it got dark. On Saturdays I'd spend the whole day playin' ball. I wouldn't even come home to eat. I've always had to watch how I played because I have heart trouble. I guess that is one reason why Dad never would let me play with the other kids.

I've never had nothin', never did expect nothin', and the good Lord has taken care of me. Riches are a burden to the spirit, and I guess the Lord knows what he was doing by never giving us much.

I've lived in this same ol' house for twelve years. The man who owns it comes by and collects the rent every month. He owns lots of houses around here. He's a crazy old man, a millionaire. He never spends a penny. That's how he got rich. He rides a bicycle and wears the same old clothes all the time. That's a rich old man.

We've always had plenty of beans in the pot and cornbread in the oven and clothes on our backs. We've never really been wantin' for anything. The Lord has been good to us.

Johnny, the one that's four, has been sick an awful lot. When my wife was pregnant with him her teeth got brittle and whitish, and it wasn't long before they started coming out. She is almost as toothless as her old Mother now. Then, after Johnny was born we had trouble after trouble with him. I guess he is going to be the unlucky child of this family. We've had him in the hospital four or five different times. This last time he was in for a month and a half, off and on. He has a hole between the two sides of his heart, and it don't pump right. The doctors thought they might have to operate. But, they didn't. They sent him home. He's got a machine and a tent that he has to stay in sometimes. And, my wife has to beat him in the chest part of every day.

The Lord always carries us through every sickness. I've spent an awful lot of time sittin' up in hospitals, prayin', and the Lord hasn't let us down yet.

### THE ANTHROPOLOGIST

The emotionally significant symbols around which people in Jake's Bottoms organize their behavior are the Lord (not the church), the family, the community (not as a structured place but as a familiar place), the mill, and fate. These symbols become the foci for the organization of a way of life that is paced by biological events. The resulting behaviors look away from the larger society in which they are meshed. Social change in terms of the larger society is not cultivated. Indeed, the world may be seen to drop off at the edge of Jake's Bottoms.

The organization of behavior is community specific, even family specific. The primary contact with the outside comes through the mass media, the mill, and schools. But, these are bothersome influences that are either encysted or ignored and seldom responded to positively. Usually the outside is associated with authority; authority that is illegitimate to community members.

This paper is an attempt to portray the major areas of symbolic behavior that are characteristic of the men and women inhabiting one urban mill village. My attempt has been to project the actual thoughts and ideas of specific individuals living there, rather than to abstract these into a terminology that sacrifices realism.

As anthropologists have turned to urban, complex societies for field research, a number of new approaches to ethnography have been tried. The work of Elliott Liebow (1967) and Oscar Lewis

(1959; 1961; 1965) demonstrate some of these approaches. Working from a community point of view has been feasible with small populations and relatively isolated groups of people. This approach seems to become more untenable as social scientists analyze the behavior of groups that are closer to their own (Valentine 1968:174). The complexities of behavior become more apparent, and perhaps more real because of the mass society. So, the search is for a unit of behavior that is feasible for observation, analysis, and realism.

In this paper I have tried to blend three goals of description: empirical, realistic, and sentient. Focusing on the actual behaviors that are generated by specific individuals seems to be the best way to achieve this blend. The individual is the unit of behaving. This is an attempt to conceptualize culture as an "existential attribute of actual men in society" (Bidney 1967:xv).

Are these behaviors typical of all the individuals who live in Jake's Bottoms? Is Jake's Bottoms typical of all lower white communities? The concept "typical" does not adequately describe the behavior here. Many life problems and assumptions about behaving are similar for lower class white people. But, the behavioral responses may vary.

Thus, the question becomes whether the behavior is generic to the group, i.e. does the behavior described come out of the cultural assumptions and premises generally used and understood in the group? Individuals generate behavior from certain cultural assumptions and premises which exist in their group (Wallace 1962:351). More than one action may be generated from one cultural assumption.

These behaviors are generic to Jake's Bottoms. Everyone in the community shares or understands both the behaviors described here and the emotionally significant symbols from which they are generated. Because of role differences a person may not be in a position to generate some behaviors. But, he will understand these behaviors sufficiently to mesh his own with them. Billy Joe may not behave like his in-laws, nor approve of their behavior, but he knows that some people are like that.

As a respectable member of his community, there are certain behaviors (excessive drunkenness, fighting, tattoos) that he may shun. But, he knows some people will do those things. The emotionally significant symbols and the behavior Billy Joe derived from them are shared by most of the respectable people. As a person becomes peripheral (either disreputable or upwardly mobile) he will increasingly generate other behaviors and acquire additional emotionally significant symbols.

Each incident, idea, and action portrayed here I have collected in the course of eighteen months of participant observation and interviewing in Jake's Bottoms. The substantive material is empirical; some of the wording and organization are mine.

## NOTES

1. I wish to thank J. Kenneth Morland and Charles Hudson for their comments on an earlier version of this paper.

2. Parts of this paper were delivered at the 68th annual meeting of the American Anthropological Association in New Orleans, Louisiana, in November 1969, under the title 'Symbolic Behavior in Urban Milltown.'

## REFERENCES

Bidney, David, 1967. *Theoretical Anthropology*, Second, augmented edition (New York: Schocken Books).

Lewis, Oscar, 1959. *Five Families* (New York: Basic Books).

———————————— 1961. *The Children of Sanchez* (New York: Random House).

Liebow, Elliot, 1967. *Tally's Corner* (New York: Little, Brown, and Co.)

Valentine, Charles, 1968. *Culture and Poverty* (Chicago: The University of Chicago Press).

Wallace, Anthony F. C., 1962. Culture and Cognition. *Science* 135: 351-357.

# Slingings and High Shots: Moonshining in the Georgia Mountains

John Gordon

Moonshining, or the making of illicit liquor, is an activity that comes to mind when one mentions mountain people; and indeed it should, for the development of illegal distilling in this country got its start in the isolated mountain areas of Appalachia.[1] The production of moonshine has now become such a large scale business in many Southern states that the federal government has, in addition to employing hundreds of Alcohol and Tobacco Tax agents, actually launched a concerted campaign (involving modern advertising techniques) aimed at drying up the production of illicit liquor in these states. Although moonshining is by no means confined to the mountain areas, it is still very much alive in the mountains and much can be learned about moonshining from the mountain people. A well developed folklore of moonshining exists in the highlands, and one can hardly spend any time there without contact with moonshining in some form.

In spite of the uniqueness of moonshining, its traditions, and its effect upon mountain subculture, little has been written on the sociological and technological aspects of the activity. Winston and Butler published an article in 1943 on Negro moonshiners in eastern North Carolina, and Loyal Durand, Jr. has written on the mountain moonshining of east Tennessee in the *Geographical Review*. The classic work by Horace Kephart, *Our Southern Highlanders*, contains two humorous chapters on the history of mountain moonshining and the state of the art in the early decades of this century. The most thorough account to date of the technology of moonshining was published in 1968 in an article by the staff writers for *Foxfire*, a quarterly magazine published by high school students in the Rabun Gap School in north Georgia.

My purpose in this paper is to briefly describe the technology of moonshining and then to examine some of its sociological and economic implications. Specifically, I shall attempt to explain the popularity of moonshining as opposed to other types of work which are safer and less demanding.

Mountain people know how to build many different types of stills; the type selected for use is determined by the speed at which the operator wants to produce and the quality desired in the final product. One of my main informants was a fifty-one year old ex-moonshiner who had begun making liquor when he was eight years old. Doc was a specialist at making the type of still known as the "blockade" or "rerun" still. Although this type of still has been one of the more popular varieties, several other kinds are often used; and the desire for quick profit with these other stills has, in many cases, resulted in a product that is not far removed from pure poison. If the blockade still is properly constructed and run with care, however, the operator can produce a liquor of very good quality.

The basic parts of the blockade still are the still itself,[2] the furnace (which is built around the still), the cap and cap stem, the thump post and thump barrel, the headache piece, the pre-heater box and trough, the slide connections, the flake stand, and the condenser. (See diagram.) After the still is constructed, the first step in the distilling process is the making of the mash, or beer, which will be run through the still. Several different "recipes" for making the beer are used by various operators. Generally, to make the mash, the operator fills the still full of water and adds the proper amount of corn meal. The furnace is fired and this mixture of meal and water is cooked. It is unnecessary to connect any of the still's parts during this procedure. The boiling mixture is then drawn out of the still into barrels or into the box dug in under the slop arm. Corn malt and rye meal are then added to the cooked meal. This starts the mixture to "working." The malt contains the enzyme diastase which saccharifies the starch of the raw corn meal. To obtain the corn malt used in this process, the moonshiner often had to sprout and grind his own corn. This complicated the distilling operation because it is a federal offense (just like moonshining itself) to grind sprouted corn. A miller who was a trusted friend was a necessity.

After the mixture has set for a day or so, it is stirred up again and sugar is added. Sugar increases the yield, but it is not used by all moonshiners because with its use the product is not considered "pure corn whiskey" (*Foxfire* 1968:102). While the mixture is fermenting, a crust or cap forms on the surface. When the mixture works off—that is, when the cap has disappeared—the beer is ready to run; the alcohol in the mixture has eaten off the crust.

When I asked Doc to give me his "recipe" for the mash, this is what he said:

O.K. John, you want me to give you a recipe how to make moonshine, so I can't write so I guess I'll just tell you how you do this and you can put it on your tape here. So the way you do that now, you get your meal, you get your still, and you put it in the furnace and you build a fire under it. So you fill it about ⅔ full of water, a fifty gallon still we'll say, a 'pacity fifty gallons. So you put a bushel a meal in it and you stir it up good with your scrape paddle. And you keep your fire under it and when it goes to boilin—then, you cap it, with the cap, and the steam comes out the stem thar. You let it boil fifteen minutes. O. K., and then you draw it over in your boxes, now that's the box that's dug in under your slop arm where you make your beer. So you push your swab stick up and you draw your beer over into the box, ah, your meal or water you've cooked, and so you have your corn malt thar and on this 38 square box you put ½ bushel of dry corn malt and a gallon of rye meal. You stir it up good, and that's in the evening, or the morning, and you let it set about twelve to twenty hours and then you go back and stir it up good and you put about one hundred pounds of sugar on this box. Then you stir it up good and go back in about twelve hours and stir it up again. And then when it works off, you, ah—when it clears off like water on top—then you put it in your still and you go to running it just like usual.

With the beer ready and the still parts connected, the operator can begin the run. A fire is built in the furnace and as the beer begins to heat, the operator must periodically stir the mixture to keep it from sticking to the bottom and sides of the still. A duck nest furnace of the type Doc builds, by recirculating its heat, is said to "burn its own smoke." This lessens the danger of discovery of the operation. After the beer has come to a boil, steam will begin to flow through the connections. From the still, steam goes through the thump barrel and headache piece into the pre-heater box. The thump barrel also contains beer, and the steam bubbling through the beer makes a deep thumping noise. The pre-heater box contains a copper ring similar to the condenser. At the beginning of the run, beer is put in the box to cover the ring. Steam going through the copper heats the beer, and when all of the beer in the still has boiled away a trough is then placed between the heater box and the uncapped still. The gate on the box is opened and the pre-heated beer flows into the still.

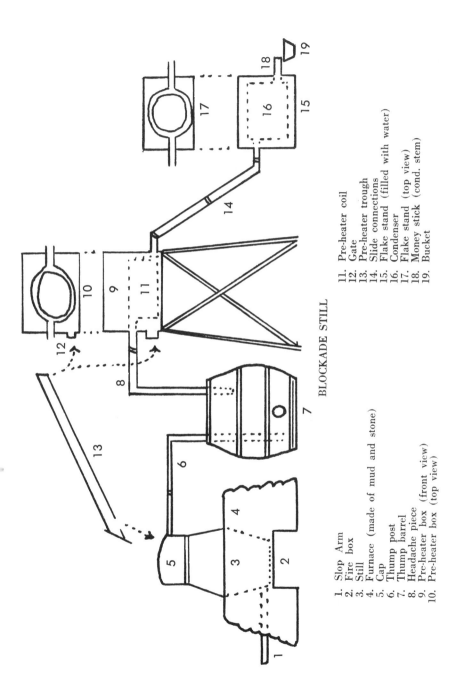

BLOCKADE STILL

1. Slop Arm
2. Fire box
3. Still
4. Furnace (made of mud and stone)
5. Cap
6. Thump post
7. Thump barrel
8. Headache piece
9. Pre-heater box (front view)
10. Pre-heater box (top view)

11. Pre-heater coil
12. Gate
13. Pre-heater trough
14. Slide connections
15. Flake stand (filled with water)
16. Condenser
17. Flake stand (top view)
18. Money stick (cond. stem)
19. Bucket

Because the beer is already hot, little time is lost waiting for the beer to boil. This makes the operation, therefore, almost continuous.

From the pre-heater box the steam goes into the flake stand. The flake stand, a wooden box similar to the pre-heater, contains the condenser. During distillation, water (usually from a nearby stream) runs through the box and condenses the steam into alcohol. The product trickles out the condenser stem and is caught in a bucket or barrel. A funnel inserted in the bucket or barrel contains a filter of charcoal wrapped in cloth which strains the fusel oils out of the alcohol.

The first run usually does not produce any whiskey strong enough to "hold a bead."[3] The product from the first run of a fifty gallon still should be about ten gallons of weak liquor. To start the next run, the still is drained and re-filled with fresh beer. The thump barrel is also emptied and the ten gallons from the first run, known as slingings or backings, are put in the thump barrel. On the second run the product will be much stronger because the steam is going through the alcohol in the thump barrel and being "doubled." The second run should produce about two gallons of good alcohol and around eight weak gallons. The weak gallons, as before, form the backings for the next run. This process is continued until all the beer is used. After about seven runs, the result will be seven to ten gallons of pure corn whiskey. This whiskey is close to 200 proof and is called "high shots."

Doc describes how he makes liquor:

So the way you do, John, you make the mash, that's in boxes as we do back in the mountains. So you cook your meal and mash it up and you put your corn malt or any kind of malt you want to on it. Well, when your beer works off, it usually takes seventy-two hours on up to three or four days according to how many hogs fall in it, and possums, so forth and so on. So anyway, John, now the way you do this, son, you fill up the still here with the beer and take the beer here and put it in this heater, it's a pre-heater, what it is, a double condenser, it's a quick way of makin' it. So why we invented this heater it's much faster and much easier, and while you rest you take off a keg of liquor and bring back a load of wood.

So, haint nothing to it, and then you fill up the heater with beers. You got a trough over here in the flake stand, you run the water right down through it, and so now what happens when it goes to boilin', you can use wood or coal or anything you want to, but we usually back in the mountains use wood, such as sourwood, fence rails, so forth and so on. So the way you do this now, when it goes to boilin', you cap it and you pour a couple a gallon of beer in your thump barrel to start off with. So then, when it goes to runnin whiskey you take up a little proof vial, we call it out there, under the condenser stem. And then you check it, you shake it down to a bead and it gets down to about 100 proof then you stop an put the bucket, a bucket's usually what we use, or a tub, or a keg, or a barrel, and you change and you catch the backings. Well the backings is a low grade of whiskey, it's alcohol, and you catch 'em as long as it burns. The way you tell, when they get weak you throw 'em under the furnace and when they blaze, they still good. So you catch what backings you get there and then you go to changin' and you switch it from one to another. And then you pour, refill it back up, and you start the same operation over and over, again and again.

So, I have the names here on this little still, very 'cular names, they true. The names on these stills, here are the slop arm, that's where the slop comes out, we call it slop, after it's boiled down into whiskey then it goes back to make re-mash again. The slop arm is where you put the swab stick, a swab stick is a mallet or a forked stick with a tow sack wrapped on it, ever body that's ever made any whiskey knows what I mean. And then we come on up to the still, and the duck nest furnace is a new model furnace that burns its own smoke. So we used to make 'em old groundhog furnaces, two or three different ways you make furnaces. But we invented this duck nest furnace, it burns its own smoke, and the man won't see you—you know how it is—you gotta be careful when you're makin it; ah, I tried to be—seven times I learnt better.

So, the way you do it, go on down the cap stem on down into the headache piece, thump post go down in the barrel and thumps the backings into processed whiskey. And why they call it a headache piece, that's the one that goes up here, John, out of the thump barrel up here into the pre-heater, and it's the headache piece now, son, and the reason I know this *is* the headache piece, if you've drunk as much of this pop-skull as I have, you'll find out exactly what I mean. Well, it goes on down and the water it runs into the slide connections, and the condenser is what condenses steam into alcohol. I'll tell you now about this condenser business, ah, we used to make 'em with old worms, coil worms, foil worms, and all that. So my grandfather invented this condenser; it's a quick, easier way to make it. So the way the whole set up goes, the pressure, John, pushes the steam through this rotation, on through the thump barrel over into the pre-heater, right on down in the condenser. And the pressure, or the temperature, is about 480 degrees, so I've been told. And the pressure from this fire pushes it right on down and the steam goes right on through all these connections, right on down through the slide connections into the condenser, and the water condenses this into liquor—alcohol—and it comes out here at the money stick.

The most frequent explanation for the popularity of moonshining in the mountains is couched in economic terms. The marginal mountain farmer, so the argument goes, can clear practically no profit from selling his poor quality corn on the open market. But when the corn is concentrated into liquor, its value jumps many times and the mountaineer can thus realize a good return. No doubt the economic factor is a very important (perhaps the most important) motivation to engage in illicit liquor production. It has certainly been stressed by those who have written on this subject, as we shall see below. It is my contention, however, that other factors must also be considered in any explanation of the appeal of moonshining. My experience suggests that were the economic factor the sole justification for moonshining, the practice would virtually die out.

Historically speaking, moonshining was greatly stimulated by economic pressures. All sources seem to agree on this. Campbell (1921:106) states that, "Moonshining is due primarily to economic reasons." Winston and Butler (1943:692) contend that the Negro moonshiners of eastern North Carolina have "drifted into the business because the amount of poor land they cultivate is not sufficient to keep them and their families employed steadily and profitably." The writers of *Foxfire* (1968:38) agree with Horace Kephart, "He [Kephart] argues most effectively that the primary reason for all this [moonshining] was economic, and we agree completely." Kephart (1913:122-123) relates his findings through the words of one of his mountain friends:

> . . . the main reason for this 'moonshining,' as you-uns calls it, is bad roads . . . . From hyar to the railroad is seventeen miles, with two mountains to cross; and you've seed that road! I recollect you-uns said every one o' them miles was a thousand rods long. . . . Seven hundred pounds is all the load a good team can haul over that road, when the weather's good. Hit takes three days to make the round trip, less'n you break an axle, and then hit takes four. When you do git to the railroad, th'r ain't no town of a thousand people within fifty mile. Now us folks ain't even got wagons. Thar's only one sarviceable wagon in this whole settlement, and you can't hire it without team and driver, which is two dollars and a half a day. . . . The only farm produce we-uns can sell is corn. You see for yourself that corn can't be shipped outen hyar. We can trade hit for store credit—that's all. Corn *juice* is about all we can tote around over the country and git cash money for. Why, man, that's the only way some folks has o' payin' their taxes!

Within the last twenty-five or thirty years a fairly extensive system of highways has penetrated Appalachia. Many areas still remain isolated, but in north Georgia the highway system is quite extensive. Now if the economic argument based on "bad roads" was valid, then moonshining should have disappeared in these areas when good roads were built. It obviously has not. One may counter, however, that the better road network simply made distribution of the product easier and therefore moonshining became more profitable. This no doubt is true. As Durand (1956:178) states, "Good roads, nearly all of them gravelled and many of them paved, have been provided by the respective states. The moonshiner is able to dispose of his product several hundred miles from its region of manufacture. . . ." The fact remains, however, that making illegal liquor is an extremely exacting, as well as a dangerous, business. Raine (1924:132) comments, "The making of moonshine is sleepless, nerve-racking work, and produces comparatively little return for the long days and nights of strain." Furthermore, in the counties where I worked, better employment (in terms of pay and less strenuous work) was available. It stands to reason, then, that the economic aspect of moonshining cannot be its sole appeal. If it were, then the moonshiners should have long ago switched over to work in the various light industries (textiles, shoes, etc.) of the area.

Why, then, do some mountain people prefer the relatively insecure life of the moonshiner to the relatively secure life of the factory worker? Winston and Butler (1943:693) have come close to what I believe may be the answer in saying that, "A small proportion of bootleggers enjoy their trade and actually get a 'thrill' out of the suspense and uncertainty and danger connected with it." They contend that this group is in the minority. But I believe this thrill factor is, on the contrary, of great importance. Winston and Butler further state that, "The manufacture and sale of bootleg whiskey is not sufficiently exciting or remunerative to induce the Negro youth to engage in such activities unless there are no alternative economic opportunities in the same community or section of the State." This observation does not hold true for the area in which I worked. As mentioned previously, better employment was available in the area to the extent that moonshining should have ceased to be a significant activity.

Herbert Gans has developed a conceptual framework which attempts to explain the type of thrill seeking behavior mentioned above in the statement by Winston and Butler. In his study of Italian-Americans in a Boston slum (1962), Gans describes the slum dwellers in terms of several differing behavior styles, the two most important categories being "action-seekers" and "routine-seekers." The routine-seeker feels comfortable when he has established a fairly definite and repetitive living pattern, such as working each day from nine to five, attending church every Sunday at 11:00, and watching the same television programs every Tuesday night. The action-seeker, at the opposite end of the spectrum, enjoys more thrilling and spontaneous activities. He tends to live episodically.

Jack Weller in *Yesterday's People* (1965:40-43) has applied Gans' concepts to the mountain people of West Virginia. Weller describes the action-seeker as one whose "jobs are often the unstable ones, or those offering excitement or change." He contends that coal mining, as a dangerous activity, appeals to those with action-seeking personalities. "Many a coal miner will leave a steady, routine factory job in the city any time to take back a job in the mines." Weller believes that mountain people as a group are predominantly more action-seeking than routine-seeking. My observations tend to support this belief, and I contend that the action-seeking personality is a characteristic of the average mountain moonshiner. Moonshining, like coal mining, is a dangerous, thrilling activity.

By this I do not mean that all moonshiners, or even all mountain moonshiners, should be considered action-seekers. I do not deny that some moonshiners are purely economically motivated. My observations indicate, however, that in most cases, something in addition to the profit motive is at work; and I suggest that it is the action-seeking aspect of the mountain personality that drives men to risk their fortunes and even their lives in the making of illegal liquor.

## NOTES

1. The original version of this paper was presented at the 1969 annual meeting of the Southern Anthropological Society in New Orleans, Louisiana. The paper itself is a modified portion of an undergraduate honors thesis written at the University of Georgia. This thesis is presently being published in four installments in *The Georgia Review;* all installments have been published to date (Gordon 1970). Permission from *The Georgia Review* to reproduce part of this material here is appreciated.

The research for the paper was conducted in the Appalachian region of Georgia during the summer of 1968. My major informant was a garrulous ex-moonshiner who was always eager to tell of his past accomplishments in the "moonshine life." He was happy to record his methods and techniques on my tape recorder, and most of my information was, therefore, collected this way. My general research method was participant-observation. I am grateful to Charles Hudson for his helpful comments.

2. The term "still" can refer to the entire unit, as in "moonshine still," or merely to the metal container in which the beer is boiled.

3. To check the strength or proof of the liquor, the operator fills a small bottle (called the proof vial) with the product and thumps the bottle in the palm of his hand. If the bubbles that rise remain steady in the center of the bottle, then the liquor is of proper strength and it is said "to hold a bead."

## REFERENCES

Campbell, John C., 1921. *The Southern Highlander and his Homeland* (New York: Russell Sage Foundation).

Durand, Loyal, 1956. Mountain Moonshining in East Tennessee. *Geographical Review* 46:168-81.

*Foxfire*, 1968. The End of Moonshining as a Fine Art. *Foxfire* 2, nos. 3 and 4.

Gans, Herbert, 1962. *The Urban Villagers* (New York: Free Press of Glencoe).

Gordon, John L., Jr., 1970. Up Top Amongst None: Life in The Georgia Appalachians. *The Georgia Review*, 24, No. 1, pp. 5-28; No. 2, pp. 183-199; No. 3, pp. 337-348; No. 4, pp. 483-494.

Kephart, Horace, 1913. *Our Southern Highlanders* (New York: Outing Publishing Co.).

Raine, James, 1924. *The Land of Saddle Bags* (Richmond, Va.: Presbyterian Committee of Publication).

Sheppard, M. E., 1935. *Cabins in the Laurels* (Chapel Hill: University of North Carolina Press).

Sherman, Mandel and Thomas R. Henry, 1933. *Hollow Folk* (New York: Thomas Y. Crowell Co.).

Weller, Jack E., 1965. *Yesterday's People: Life in Contemporary Appalachia* (Lexington: University of Kentucky Press).

Winston, Sanford and Mosette Butler, 1943. Negro Bootleggers in Eastern North Carolina. *American Sociological Review* 8:692-7.

# How to Lose the Hounds: Technology of the Gullah Coast Renegade

H. Eugene Hodges

THE Gullah Coast is a distinctive cultural area noted in the literature for its richness in folklore and folk music. It encompasses the geographical area from Charleston, South Carolina to Kingsland, Georgia and includes the offshore islands, the pine forests, and swamps of the coastal plains. While interviewing in a rural section in this area, I discovered a social type designated by members of the community as "renegades". The first time I heard the term "renegade" was during an interview session with an informant whose primary source of income was the manufacture of illegal whiskey. When the interview session was concluded and I was about to leave, I asked my informant for directions to Mr. X's house. My informant became visibly upset and responded, "You ought not to go to those people's house. They're a bunch of renegades." I did not attach any significance to the term, but I was curious about the reason for his hostility towards Mr. X. When I asked him what he meant by renegade, he gave me a rather confusing description of a person who lives outside the law. Since he himself was a moonshiner, his explanation made little sense to me.

During an interview with another informant I again brought Mr. X into the conversation. The response was "If you are going to visit that family you better not go by yourself. Those people are renegades." It was at this point that I began to see that perhaps I had uncovered a social type. I postponed my visit to Mr. X's house until I could discover what a renegade was. The definition which emerged was that the renegade is, first of all, a person who has broken the law and has been found out. But this in itself was certainly not unusual in the population I was studying. Most of my informants were making their living by either illegal fishing or by moonshining. The thing that made the renegade distinctive was that when he became a fugitive from the law, he ran to the swamps, the pine forest, or the offshore islands where he remained isolated from the necessities of civilization and feared by members of the community. In contrast, when other members of the community became fugitives, they would leave the county to reside in one of the fishing communities in Savannah, Charleston, or Jacksonville.

Two families were designated as a "bunch of renegades" by my informants. The label seemed to apply not only to specific members of the family but to the entire family. And of these two families there was no living member who had actually been a renegade. The renegade label meant only that the family had produced renegades in the past but the last renegade anyone could name lived in the area about 1915. This renegade was related to Mr. X and was described as a real renegade, who, when the hounds were after him, would drink cow's blood by cutting the vein on a cow's neck, drinking his fill, and then sealing the vein back up by pressing on it. "He would just keep on running."

The content of this paper is from separate interviews with the male heads of the two renegade families. In no instance did either of the two informants mention specific members of their families who were renegades in the past, and after several "polite" attempts to probe this met with failure, I let it drop. The interviews were characterized by an easy, flowing conversation in which I played the part of an interested listener, asking questions to direct the informant to particular subjects. The two families knew each other by name and sight, but had never interacted. But both informants knew how to lose the hounds and "how to live out there." The combination of these two bodies of knowledge is what I refer to as "the technology of the renegade"; it includes techniques of food gathering, food preservation, and cooking as well as the procedure for losing the hounds. The focus of this paper is on the procedure for losing the hounds which the sheriff placed on the fugitive's trail.

## LOSING THE HOUNDS

The renegade's strategy for losing the hounds is based on a number of "tricks" or ploys which are designed for particular purposes. There are tricks designed solely to lose the hounds, but are not expected to confuse the sheriff. There are tricks designed to exhaust the hounds, and tricks designed to confuse, exhaust, and lose the hounds as well as the sheriff.

Once the hounds are placed on the renegade's scent, the renegade perceives that he is locked in combat with not one, but two rather formidable opponents. First of all there are the hounds themselves, which have the ability to follow an invisible scent, which can run at least three times faster than a man, and which have tremendous stamina. In addition they have a voice, a bark which relays to the sheriff information such as the direction of the fugitive's flight or contact with the fugitive. But, the hounds by themselves are the least of the renegade's problems. It is the sheriff, referred to by the renegade as "the Man," the human intelligence behind the hounds, who is the major opponent. In the renegade's words, "Any damn fool can outsmart a hound, but you have to lose the Man behind the hounds to be home free." It is with this definition of the situation that the renegade joins combat.

When the hounds pick up the fugitive's scent, the sheriff and his posse will not follow behind the hounds, but will attempt to follow the hounds' barking in their automobiles as long as the roads permit. When the hounds are on the scent, their barking takes on a muffled quality as a result of their noses being almost on the ground. The hounds will also be in a tight pack, barking in unison and moving swiftly. If the hounds lose the scent, the pack will disperse, attempting to pick up the scent, the barking will be irregular, and the muffled quality will be absent. The hounds will mill around, roughly in the same spot, until they are put back on the scent. If the hounds catch the fugitive on the ground, they will attack and hold the fugitive at bay. In such a case the noise produced will be unmistakably clear. But generally the fugitive will climb a tree to avoid being caught on the ground and injured. In this case the hounds bark the "treed" bark which is characterized by a long, hollow howl. The hollow quality is due to the hounds' heads being skyward as they are looking up into the tree.

The significance of the hounds' voice is that the sheriff does not have to follow on foot behind the hounds, but can remain on the ridge roads, and by interpreting the hounds' bark he can follow in an automobile. He can also anticipate the direction of flight and head the fugitive off. The renegade is aware of this and will change directions at irregular intervals to avoid being headed off. He also knows that as long as the Man is on the ridge road "sitting high, dry, and rested," he will have to keep running forever. One part of the renegade's strategy is to exhaust the sheriff: "He'll call off the hounds when he's had enough." One informant explained how to do this: "You have to keep the Man off the hill, in the swamp, wet and working." Any simple trick which can lose the hounds will require the sheriff to leave the hill and walk the distance to where the hounds are in order to place them back on the scent. For example, the renegade may find two trees which are in contact so that he is able to climb up one tree, cross over, and climb down the other. The hounds will follow the scent to the tree and voice the "treed" bark. When the sheriff arrives, he will instantly see what has happened and place the hounds back on the scent. But in the meantime the renegade has accomplished two things: he has gained the extra time it takes for the sheriff to walk from the hill to the trick, and the sheriff is no longer sitting high and dry on the ridge road, but is now "wet and working."

The renegade repeats this trick every time the situation presents itself and the sheriff and posse fall in behind the hounds to add the now necessary commodity of human intelligence to the chase. The renegade had gained time to rest and the added time to pull off a more elaborate trick, one designed to fool both the hounds and the sheriff.

It seems to be the popular opinion that all one has to do to lose the hounds is to run into a stream, but this disregards the fact that there is human intelligence behind the hounds. In a situation where a fugitive destroys his scent by wading in a stream the posse searches both sides of the stream and finds where the futigive exits and then places the hounds back on the scent. The renegade's tricks take this into consideration, and he therefore attempts to confuse the Man as well as to lose the hounds.

It should be noted at this point that the renegade seems to be working on the basis of something on the order of a folk psychology. His perception of the view of himself in the eyes of the other becomes an instrument which he uses to aid in his escape. A clear example of this came to light when the discussion touched upon the stream trick. Both informants agreed that upon entering the stream the fugitive should at first go with the current, not against the current, because "the Man always thinks that you are lazy and that you'll take the easiest way."

When the hounds lose the scent at the stream, the Man will at first go with the current expecting to find the exit path in that direction. The renegade goes with the current several hundred feet and exits on the opposite side of the stream. After running through the woods for a way, the renegade will re-enter the stream and wade further down stream and exit on the opposite side from the one he has just entered. The object of these maneuvers is that once the first exit is found the sheriff will have to carry or drag the hounds across the stream in order to place them on the scent, and this has to be repeated each time a new exit is found. This, of course, is consistent with the strategy of keeping the Man wet and working.

The number of exits and false trails which the renegade leaves is dependent upon the amount of time and energy he possesses. He knows something of the amount of time he has, for he too can hear the hounds.

Upon making the final entrance into the stream, the renegade double tracks against the current and passes his original entrance. Now he goes as far up stream as he has time and exits without leaving visible signs. To do this, he looks for an overhanging limb by which he can pull himself into a tree without setting foot on the bank. When he jumps from the tree he attempts to land as far away from the water's edge as possible, for it is at the water's edge that the sheriff and the hounds are patrolling. If he can put distance between the water's edge and his exit from the tree, he may be home free. However, if the Man is persistent he may still pick up the trail, but it will take considerable time for the Man to handle this trick, and the renegade has time to rest and prepare for the next round.

In passing, my informant noted that the final exit from the stream had to be a great distance from the first false exit, because if the posse happened to be very large, it could be split into four groups, and both sides of the stream could be covered in both directions. But when the first false exit is found, the smaller groups will be called together, and the chase will be carried in that direction.

Another trick designed to exhaust the hounds and lose the Man can be performed if the renegade happens upon a field fence. The procedure in this trick is to cross the fence, but double back and cross to the other side again. He lays down a false trail parallel to the fence and again cuts back to the fence. He climbs and walks the fence back to the middle of his previous parallel trail. He then exits from the fence and makes a new trail out from the fence to his parallel trail and then retracks his other entrance back to the fence. This lays down so many overlapping trails that both the hounds and the Man are confused. If the renegade has time he may just walk the fence, jumping off each time on the side opposite to his last exit, laying down false trails, but always doubling back to the fence. This last trick was given as one which will wear out the hounds. While a man may not expend much energy climbing a fence, the hounds have a great deal of difficulty. The object of the trick is to make the hounds cross the fence as many times as possible. This trick was considered to be especially effective in exhausting leashed bloodhounds and exhausting the hound's master, who has to constantly lift the animal across the fence.

The final exit from the fence should be made in the same manner as the exit from the stream, by means of an overhanging limb or by simply jumping as far as possible from the fence. Again it will be at the edge of the fence that the Man will be looking for the exit.

In the event that the renegade happens upon an area of hard ground in which he will not leave footprints, he is prepared with a special trick. This trick involves laying down a false trail for several hundred feet and retracing his steps. He then repeats this at least twice, taking care to stay on his original trail as best he can. Once he has laid down a strong scent by means of this double tracking, the renegade starts down the trail again but begins to veer from the original trail so that he ends up a hundred or so feet away from the end of his false trail. He then takes off running. This trick is designed to lose both the hounds and the Man. The hounds will take the strongest scent, and when they reach the end of the false trail they will retrack, but will again take the stronger of the two scents. And since this trick occurred on hard ground which does not leave footprints, the Man may be unable to perceive what has happened.

From the minute that the renegade knows that the hounds are on his trail, he begins to look for something which will "wear out the hounds' nose." This involves rubbing on the bottom of his shoes something which would destroy the hounds' ability to smell. Wild onions or turnips repeatedly rubbed on the shoe soles were said to wear out the hounds' nose. One informant mentioned that if you happened to run across a skunk, "just go up and kick him in the butt and there ain't no hound in Georgia that'll follow you."

It is significant that a large array of household goods were mentioned, such as red or black pepper, pine-oil and turpentine; kerosene and gasoline were also considered effective in destroying a hound's sense of smell. At the very time a person becomes a fugitive, the commodities of civilization take on new and instrumental significance. This is the point at which a bottle of pine-oil is perceived as being the difference between life or death, freedom or imprisonment, and the difference between a picturesque character and a desperate man becomes clear.

Perhaps this in some way explains the antipathy found in the community towards this type of deviant. When the renegade becomes isolated from the commodities of civilization but chooses to continue living in the geographical area, perhaps he can realistically be perceived as a serious threat. One informant in the community referred to a renegade as a person who would "kill you for the nails in your shoes" and then added, "or for your boat." The renegade is perceived not so much as a killer but as a desperate person.

## CONCLUSION

The purpose of this paper has been to call attention to the existence of a social type who is so much on the fringe that he possesses a specialized technology for avoidance of capture by the law. The possession of such a technology implies a degree of alienation which one would not expect to find among indigenous, white, Southern people. However, it is not only present, it is several generations deep. The cause of this alienation, then, cannot be credited to the recent encroachment of industry and the means of mass production upon a simple and unassuming folk way of life. This alienation also existed in the agrarian society of the late 1800s.

There is another interesting aspect of the alienation of the two renegade families which should be pointed out. The renegade informants considered themselves alienated from society and this was manifested in their possession of a technology for avoiding capture. This is alienation in a strict sociological sense, in that sociology treats the alienated person as being aware of his alienation. But the renegade's alienation does not take a revolutionary form. It is more like the "amoral familism" Edward Banfield (1958) found in South Italy, a moral system characterized by the belief that any act which is committed by a family member or any act which promotes the family's interest is justifiable. If the renegade's stance towards the larger society is seen as being basically anti-social, then it must be seen as being completely so, and the renegade can best be described as a person who will take a shot at any passing army, be it Federal or Revolutionary.

A question which remains to be answered is how this detailed information entailed in the procedure for losing the hounds could have been maintained in a family even though the procedure has not been used in over 50 years. A partial answer can be found in the fact that this information was passed down by means of the oral tradition, which stresses the spoken word above and beyond the written word. The oral tradition is one in which the form of communication, as opposed to the content, becomes almost an end in itself. The stories which are part of the oral tradition become structured through innumerable repetitions, and the story eventually assumes a form in which one theme leads into the next in such a smooth and easy manner that any attempt to diminish its content interrupts the pattern and distracts from the story. Therefore, even though the content is subordinate to the form, the content can be quite detailed in nature and yet remain unmodified in the innumerable retellings of the story.

The two renegade informants presented the information in the true style of the oral tradition, but unfortunately I did not use a tape recorder and I am consequently unable to reproduce the "telling" of the procedure in the manner in which the informants relayed the information to me. Only occasionally do I include the neat and precise statements which are characteristic of the oral tradition. For example, "you have to keep the Man off the hill, in the swamp, wet and working" is such a statement.

As mentioned earlier, the procedure for losing the hounds is only one aspect of the technology of the avoidance of capture which the renegades possess. Even though the many procedures of the technology are not a monopoly of the renegade families, I suspect that the manner in which they have organized all of the components necessary to avoid capture is unique. I would also hypothesize that the procedure for losing the hounds was developed originally by the field slaves on the large rice plantations in the area and that the renegade families are just the carriers of the body of knowledge. The suggestion that the renegades themselves did not originate the technology does not diminish the significance of the fact that in the second half of the twentieth century my informants still considered the technology relevant to their situation.

## REFERENCES

Banfield, Edward C., 1958. *The Moral Basis of a Backward Society* (Glencoe, Ill.: The Free Press).

# The Hippie Ghetto

William L. Partridge

The hippie ghetto in which I was a participant and observer is located in the low-rent fringe area between the white and Negro sections of a small southern town.[1] The main industry of the town is the large state university; signs at the city limits say "Welcome to University City." The residents of the ghetto are all either students or former students. They are adolescent to young adult in age, of middle class background, of both sexes, and white. The population numbered on the average about forty to fifty in 1967 and 1968, although it should be noted that it was expanding rapidly and that there were other areas of the town in which hippies lived.[2] The majority of the residents are transient, staying in the area for perhaps a year or more and then moving.

In the spring of 1967 I became interested in the phenomenon labeled as the "hippie movement" by the media and moved into the neighborhood called the "ghetto" by the students who lived there. As a participant and observer I was concerned with recording the movement of ghetto residents through time and space, the fluctuating levels of interaction intensity, and the events which defined and gave meaning to their lives.[3] Some of the conclusions which can be drawn from this study and their anthropological implications are the subject of this paper.

First, the social process of hippie ghetto life will be described as a rite of passage in which the nature of the ghetto and the relationship of the ghetto to the larger American society are defined. In this way the hippie ghetto is understood within the context of an ongoing cultural process and not simply in terms of flat, often pejorative, statements about characteristics. The ghetto will then be viewed from the perspective of the revitalization process. Certain similarities and differences between the data examined here and Wallace's (1956) processual structure will be noted. Attention will be given the role of the prophet in revitalization movements.

The hippie movement is a peculiarly American phenomenon, although it does have political counterparts in France, Japan, and other modern industrial nations (Califano 1970:60-61). It is common to refer to students on university campuses throughout the world as "alienated" and involved in youth movements. The extent to which hippies can be called alienated is of importance. The group studied here is disconnected from American society in a physical, psychological, and social sense. The name used by residents to identify their neighborhood, the "ghetto," expresses the depth of this separation. Psychologists (Keniston 1960:56) have noted the inclusive or total nature of the alienated mental state, embracing not only the self, others, and society, but the very structure of the universe and the nature of knowledge, i.e. the total cultural *Gestalt*. At the level of observable behavior it can be seen that interaction in the straight world is largely irrelevant to residents of the ghetto. Newspapers, magazines, television sets, and so on are scarce. Interaction takes place almost entirely within a tightly defined social network. The most credible sources of information are the subjective views of the novelist and the experiences of fellow residents. These are credible because it is the reader or listener who judges credibility. And credibility is important if one is to see the world "as it really is."

The continuing estrangement of hippies from American society is partly a function of the continuing rejection and condemnation which they experience. *Reader's Digest* (January 1968:59) put it this way: "Murder, Rape, Disease, Suicide. . . . The dark side of the Hippie moon has become increasingly visible." But such campaigns only partly account for the mental state of alienation. To paraphrase Goffman (1961:148), hippie behavior must be understood not only in terms of interaction with straight society but as a product of the social arrangements which evolve among hippies in response to straight society. And these social arrangements are best understood from the perspective of the natural history method (Arensberg and Kimball 1965:4-5).

By observing the social life of ghetto residents through time and space it becomes evident that the social process of ghetto life is born of the educational institution in American society. This is not to say that the phenomenon is a product of American educational institutions, but rather to say that it is a product of the role education plays in the larger American society. That role is defined here as a rite of passage, a ceremony which eases transition from one status to another (Chapple and Coon 1942:285; Turner 1969:69). The rite has three stages: separation, liminality, and incorporation. First, the initiate leaves his previous status, ceasing previous patterns of interaction and structured behaviors appropriate to that status. He moves from the confines of the nuclear family and the high school peer group into a university where he initiates new and often foreign patterns of interaction. Second, upon separation he begins a period of liminality or limbo in which his status is no longer "son of _____" or "daughter of _____" but simply student or neophyte. Along with other neophytes of differing ages, talents, and backgrounds he learns new behaviors and the traditional knowledge of "elders." He is held in this state of limbo for a specified period of time during which he experiences various tests and examinations which he must pass before he is allowed to exit. Third, the rite is completed when individuals leave the educational institution and take on a new status, different from both previous ones, which incorporates them into the larger society (Kimball and McClellen 1962).

The hippie ghetto population, then, consists of liminal individuals or students who consciously involve themselves in seeking alternatives to the larger society, or more accurately, in seeking alternatives to the status for which the educational rite has prepared them. They evolve for themselves systems of interaction which make the discovery of alternatives possible. Hippie life can be understood as a secondary rite of passage out of the large institutionalized American rite known as education.

This secondary rite, as is true of the primary one, is marked by the three stages of separation, liminality, and incorporation. First, the initiate moves out of the university and the larger society, cutting his ties with parents and friends. Second, no longer bound by the responsibilities, structured behaviors, and values associated with his previous status, he enters the stage of liminality. During this stage he begins interaction in a new social network, entering a variety of tentative associational groups made up of fellow neophytes and "elders" of the ghetto. Problems of subsistence, sex, housing, and so forth are now solved in the context of the elder-neophyte relationship as those with more experience in the subculture are able to offer assistance and support to the neophyte. The solutions to these problems often spark the formation of new associational groups based upon the male-female relationship. And third, the rite of passage is complete when the individual is incorporated into one of the several groups who have discovered some feasible adjustment to the larger society.

Turner's (1968; 1969) extended treatment of the second stage of the rite of passage is useful here, for it is the liminal period and its distinctive symbols which have caught the attention of the media. The state of liminality is characterized by "structural impoverishment and symbolic enrichment" (Turner 1968:567). Symbols of a previous status are cast off and insignia which are wholly unintelligible to former associates are taken on. More significant, perhaps, than shoulder length hair on males and hemlines which fall at the pubic area of females is the absence of structured, differentiated, hierarchical behavior and the presence of "undifferentiated *comitatus* (Turner 1969:96). I prefer using a different Latin word *comitas*, meaning politeness, civility, and kindness. Spontaneity is the vehicle for self-discovery, for being fully alive and fully human. All manner of behavior is "beautiful" if it is understood to represent a spontaneous eruption of the self. Even hostile and aggressive acts are received in the spirit of *comitas*, for they teach an individual about himself and others; not only are they welcomed but they are encouraged since they are interpreted as evidence of trust in one's fellows and commitment to what two sociologists have seen as a "quest for self-knowledge" (Simon and Trout 1967:52).

Liminality is "essentially a period of returning to first principles and taking of the cultural inventory" (Turner 1968:577). Spontaneity and experimentation deliver a host of stimuli heretofore sublimated by the demands of a previous status and structure. For to be outside of a particular social position, to be in a state of limbo, is to cease to have a specific perspective.

> [It is] in a sense to become (at least potentially) aware of all positions and arrangements and to have a total perspective. What converts potential understanding into real gnosis is instruction (Turner 1968:577).

The kaleidoscope of new stimuli is transmuted into knowledge and imbued with meaning through ceremonial communication with elders. Urges, fantasies, and fears press for recognition; these may spark insights and as such are encouraged and even directly produced by ceremonial sacraments and ceremonial behaviors. A "good head" is someone who uses drugs for the purpose of self-discovery, according to Davis and Munoz (1968:160).

The period of liminality is a time of freedom, a time when the normal moral codes have little validity and are transgressed (Turner 1969:577). Sexual relationships are not binding; friendships do not imply responsibility, and interactions fluctuate with need and temperament rather than custom. For example, the individual who is ejected from the associational group is the one who seeks to formalize and organize relationships by virtue of moral codes and sanctions. Those who transcend the moral codes of straight society remain secure in liminal freedom. Likewise, the essence of a bad trip with LSD is the inability to give in freely to the effects of the drug and the reliance upon traditional mechanisms of control in an effort to avoid unfamiliar stimuli.

It is in the nightly rites of intensification (Chappel and Coon 1942:507) of the associational group that one finds natural expressions of liminal symbols. Feelings of *comitas* are induced by ritual acts, such as sharing the sacramental drug and voicing expressions of satisfaction and contentment, and by ritual beliefs, such as the expectation that the sacrament will produce a shared psychic state in which all the participants are drawn together. Ordinary communication is held in abeyance while ceremonial communication symbolizes "honesty," a truer expression of the self, or in Turner's (1969:103) more lyrical words, "whole men in relation to other whole men." And it is in the nightly rituals that the mythology of the associational group is aired. Stories involving "ancestors" who have since moved on are related, linking those present to the almost legendary individuals whose adventures and exploits return to the ghetto through the grapevine of travelers. At a later time these may have practical value to the neophyte in that many alternatives to the larger society are revealed, but much of their significance in the rite of passage lies in their ontological value. For liminal wisdom "refashions the very being of the neophyte" and infuses him with the power to make a transition or change (Turner 1968:577). Cloaked in nonresponsibility, innocent of guilt or shame, invulnerable to the threats that stem from moral sanctions, the individual is prepared to leave the ghetto.

This second stage of the rite of passage is particularly complex and lengthy. It may last for only a few months or for several years. There are two reasons for this. First, the belief in the ideal of self-fulfillment, as evidenced by the quest for self-knowledge, demands experimentation. Solutions to problems, then, are often tentative. Secondly, the neophyte is made aware of a great number of alternatives to straight society in terms of sex, subsistence, residence patterns, and so forth. These are primary areas for self-fulfillment; a certain degree of adjustment and readjustment must take place since the population is largely transient. Movement into the third stage, incorporation, is not possible until one knows the nature of the self and how to go about fulfilling his own demands and urges.

The third stage of the rite of passage appears to be fragmented, for there are various alternatives open to the ghetto resident. Upon leaving the ghetto he may enter a variety of subcultural associational networks which may lead him to Boston, Atlanta, New York, Taos, Denver, Miami, and many other cities and towns. Some residents move to communal farms, others move to university education once again. Still others may innovate businesses, marketing the trappings of the subculture. Others may join the networks of drug dealers and learn one of the most lucrative of the alternate means of survival. And some seek out addictive drugs which work to separate them even further from straight society. It is apparent, however, that the rite does not smoothly deliver up all neophytes to a single subculture, nor does it prohibit part-time commitment to several.

Building upon this description of the social processes of hippie ghetto life, it is now possible to go on to a consideration of theoretical interpretations. It is apparent even upon cursory examination that those who seek to discover alternatives to straight society, to obtain knowledge of the self, and to live a more satisfying life are making an effort at revitalization. As defined by Wallace (1956:265), a revitalization movement is a "deliberate, organized, conscious effort by members of a society to construct a more satisfying culture."

Wallace (1956:269) indicates that revitalization efforts grow out of conditions of chronically high individual stress in which major stress-reducing techniques appear worthless. "Admission that a major [stress-reducing] technique is worthless is extremely threatening because it implies that the whole mazeway system may be inadequate" (Wallace 1956:269). The mazeway is the "total *Gestalt*" of one individual, "his image of self, society, and culture, of nature and body, and of ways of action" (Wallace 1956:267). One will note the similarity between the psychological characteristics of alienation (Keniston 1960:56) and Wallace's conception of mazeway reformulation. Likewise, Turner (1969:121) has called attention to the "peculiar linkages between personality, universal values, and 'spirit' or 'soul' that appear to be the stigmata of communitas." The period of increased individual stress is followed by a period of cultural distortion in which,

> Rigid persons apparently prefer to tolerate high levels of chronic stress rather than make systematic adaptive changes in the mazeway. More flexible persons try out various limited mazeway changes in their personal lives, attempting to reduce stress by addition or substitution of mazeway elements with more or less concern for the *Gestalt* of the system (Wallace 1956:269).

Revitalization actually begins after this period of mazeway reformulation. Wallace (1956:270) notes that in all cases with which anthropologists are familiar mazeway reformulation occurs "as a moment of insight" to a prophet or "in one or several hallucinatory visions by a single individual" in which the supernatural explains current troubles as resulting from the violation of certain rules. The prophet then reveals his insights to potential converts as doctrine and organizes his followers; the doctrine is adapted to the resistance such efforts inevitably meet, transforms the culture, and finally is routinized (Wallace 1956:273-74).

Of particular interest in the present context is the role of the prophet, for one finds little evidence of prophets in the hippie ghetto. Ritual behaviors and beliefs engage the neophyte in the "quest for self-knowledge" or personal vision seeking, but no single vision points the way to doctrine and no single person is treated with special respect in this regard. There are only "elders" in the ghetto who by virtue of longevity command a great knowledge of the mythology of the associational group and who are known to have confronted previously many of the problems which may appear new and frightening to the neophyte. Elders may act as guides or models, but their "teaching" does not involve well defined practices and programs through which the good life may be achieved. Moreover, the paths out of the ghetto are numerous and most are forked; so in this sense each individual must choose his own alternatives according to the promptings of the self and the knowledge of the experiences of others gained from the "elders."

The hippie ghetto, therefore, probably represents the period of cultural distortion in the revitalization process structure. The rite of passage may function for those who return to the larger society as "milieu therapy," much the same as Werner (1963:259-67) has observed in the case of student religious centers. This is implied, in any case, since some adjustment of the cultural *Gestalt* must take place if those who were formerly alienated now find the straight world palatable. Still, incorporation into the larger society is not desired for a significant number. And those who seek and find viable alternatives to the larger society will probably rise in number in proportion to the level of stress and distortion which they experience. The rite of passage will then deliver up the majority of those who pass through the ghetto into a revitalization movement, and the "elders" of an earlier time will become prophets.

## NOTES

1. My role as researcher was ambiguous for several reasons, foremost of which was the fact that I was a student and knew many of the residents previous

to the period of study. I identified myself as an anthropology student doing research for my MA thesis. This created no obstacles until I encountered a network of drug dealers who handled and used heroin. Access to these groups was of course denied. By moving into the ghetto area and fully participating in the subculture I became a participant.

2. This situation changed dramatically during the time I lived in the area; so dramatically that by the time I was ready to leave I would estimate that the population had doubled several times over. My sample is bounded in time, 1967-1968, and is geographically limited to the area known as the ghetto during that time.

3. While the method used was that of community studies, after Arensberg and Kimball (1965), the area and population studied can not be defined as a community in terms of the criterion that three generations be present.

## REFERENCES

Arensberg, Conrad M. and Solon T. Kimball, 1965. *Culture and Community* (New York: Harcourt, Brace, and World, Inc.).

Califano, Joseph A. Jr., 1970. *The Student Revolution: A Global Confrontation* (New York: W. W. Norton and Company).

Chapple, Elliott D. and Carleton S. Coon, 1942. *Principles of Anthropology* (New York: Holt, Rhinehart, and Winston).

Davis, Fred and Laura Munoz, 1968. Patterns and Meanings of Drug Use Among Hippies. *Journal of Health and Social Behavior* 9:156-64.

Goffman, Erving, 1961. Asylums (New York: Doubleday and Company, Inc.).

Keniston, Kenneth, 1960. *The Uncommitted: Alienated Youth in American Society* (New York: Harcourt, Brace, and World, Inc.).

Kimball, Solon T. and James E. McClellen Jr., 1962. *Education and and the New America* (New York: Randon House).

Simon, Geoffery and Grafton Trout, 1967. Hippies in College—From Teeny-boppers to Drug Freaks. *Transaction* 5:27-32.

Turner, Victor W., 1968. Myth and Symbol. *International Encyclopedia of the Social Sciences* (Macmillan Company and the Free Press).

————————, 1969. *The Ritual Process: Structure and Anti-structure* (Chicago: Aldine).

Wallace, Anthony F. C., 1956. Revitalization Movements. *American Anthropologist* 52:264-81.

Werner, Fred, 1963. Acculturation and Milieu Therapy in Student Transition. In *Education and Culture*, George D. Spindler, ed. (New York: Holt, Rhinehart, and Winston).

# A Remnant Indian Community:
# The Houma of Southern Louisiana

MAX E. STANTON

THE federal census of 1960 reported over 2,000 Indians living in the coastal marsh and swamp areas of southern Louisiana, most of whom were living along the bayous which fan out toward the Gulf of Mexico from the city of Houma.[1] Terrebonne Parish had a total of 1,980 Indians, and another 241 Indians were reported in Lafourche Parish, most of them near Bayou Lafourche, which is the boundary between the two parishes.

There is no collective name used by these people to identify themselves other than "Indian." The word "Sabine" is sometimes used, but in a derogatory sense. They prefer to be called Indians and resent, even among themselves, those who use the term Sabine. In the historical and descriptive literature, they are often referred to as Houma Indians, but this researcher was not able to find any Indians who used this designation, although some have heard it used by non-Indians. For the sake of brevity and clarity, "Houma" and "Indian" will be used interchangeably throughout this report to refer to these people.

## HISTORICAL SETTING

There is a historical connection between the present Indians of southern Louisiana and the traditional Houma Tribe. Until the eighteenth century, the Houma lived along the Mississippi River in what is now the border area of the states of Louisiana and Mississippi (Swanton 1911:285). In the first decade of the eighteenth century they were reduced in population by warfare with other Indian groups and by disease. As a result, they fled down the Mississippi to seek a more secure place in which to live. They spent the next one hundred years in the swamps of Ascension Parish, west and south of the Mississippi

82

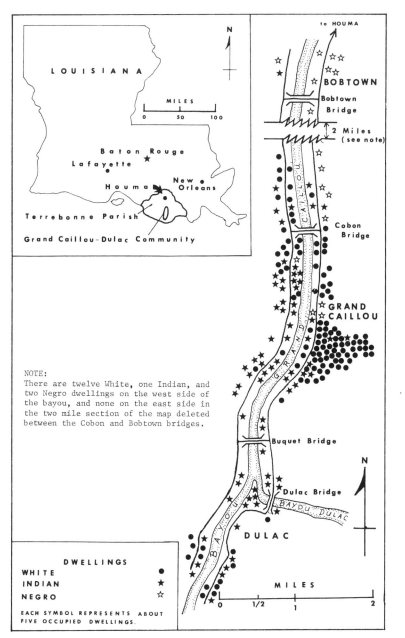

Figure 1. The Grand Caillou-Dulac Community: the approximate location of dwellings showing the ethnic identity of the occupants. The scale of the map does not allow for the actual spatial placement of each individual dwelling. Isolated symbols represent, in a few isolated cases, one or two more or one or two less than five dwellings.

River. During this time, they were joined by remnants of other tribes. Most of the new arrivals spoke Muskogean languages closely related to the Houma dialect (Swanton 1911:292). Escaped Negro slaves and Europeans (mostly French trappers and some fugitives from the law and from the military) were also accepted into the group.

In the latter part of the 1700s, French refugees from Acadia (the present-day Maritime Provinces of Canada) began to settle in southern Louisiana.[2] Some of them took Indian wives. A record dated 1795 states that land in the southern portion of Terrebonne Parish was granted to French settlers who had married local Indians (Parenton and Pellegrin 1950:149).

In the early part of the nineteenth century, large tracts of land in southern Louisiana were cleared and drained for planting sugar. Negro slaves were brought in to work on these plantations. The influx of French refugees from Acadia and the creation of large plantations brought an end to the isolation of the Houma. The main body of the tribe moved back up to the Mississippi River and have become lost to the historical record. Three bands are known to have moved into the present area of Terrebonne Parish (Swanton 1911:292). The present city of Houma was established in 1834, taking its name from a group of Houma Indians living in the vicinity. The present Indians of the area are presumed to be descendants of this Houma group.

As pressures for land and living space became more demanding, the Indians were forced to move into the brackish marsh and swamp country adjacent to the Gulf of Mexico. It was fortunate that this land was thought to be (at the time) useless by the non-Indian population, for these people were not seafarers and they had reached land's end. The sojourn in Ascension Parish had conditioned the Houma to a life of hunting, fishing, and trapping in swampy land, and they survived where others could not.

The isolation of these remaining Houma Indians was brought to an abrupt end in the late 1920s when oil and natural gas were discovered under their land. Being largely illiterate, disfranchised, and impoverished, the Houma quickly lost their rights to the now valuable land (Fischer 1968). They also were never formally associated with the federal or state government, so they were denied even what little help such formal recognition might have given them.[3]

As a result of an upset in the balance in the ecosystem by the oil companies, the fauna of the marshes and swamps began to decline. The Indians could no longer make a living in their scattered homesteads. They began to congregate in settlements at the termini of the roads along the bayous. Here they found occasional work in the oil fields, in the newly established fish and shrimp canneries, and on the commercial fishing boats. They could also supplement their income as part-time hunters and trappers and as guides for sportsmen.

By congregating into their six present locations, the Indians have become part of a larger socio-cultural unit.[4] None of these communities were unsettled before the Indians moved in, for there were Whites (mostly Cajun French) and Negroes living there as well. Of the six communities, only one, the small and semi-isolated Champs Charles (Isle St. Jean Charles), has a majority of Indian residents. Over half of all the Indians in the area live in or near Dulac on Bayou Grand Caillou, about twenty miles south of the city of Houma. There are sections in these communities, especially Dulac, which have Indian majorities, but there is no strict residential segregation. Indians, Whites, and Negroes can be found living as neighbors.

No such organization as a Houma Indian Tribal Council or any similar body representing all of the Houma exists, and there is no strong feeling of tribal or intra-group unity. The Houma live in the six communities mentioned above and have only limited contact with each other. There is, however, some small degree of inter-community contact as a result of the recent consolidation of the Terrebonne Parish high school system and the construction of new all-weather roads which offer fast and direct routes between the settlements.

## PRESENT SITUATION

Today the Indian stands as middleman in a three-tiered hierarchy, with the White (mostly Cajun French) occupying the level above and the Negro the level below. These groups live in close geographical proximity but have only limited inter-group contacts. The situation is not (as yet) tense or marked by hate and strife, but it is not one of accord either. Jealousy, discontent, scorn, and rejection are not far below the surface.

The Indians have mixed with the other two racial elements in the community, but there is strong evidence to refute claims of substantial Negro ancestry among the Houma (Roy 1959:120). Speck (1943: 215) states that they have some Spanish-French, English, and other White progenitors with no reference made to Negro admixture. He is quoted by Fischer as having said:

> In my judgment, as based upon comparisons with Indians of the southeastern tribes over a number of years, I should rate the Houma as a people possessing Indian blood and cultural characters to a degree about equal to that of the Creek, Choctaw, Catawbe [*sic*], and Seminoles (Fischer 1968:135).

It is not to be denied that these people do have some degree of Negro ancestry, but this element is not as strong as has been inferred in some earier works (such as Parenton and Pellegrin 1950: 148). As a result of racial mixing, many Indians are phenotypically indistinguishable from many Whites or Negroes in the area, but because of their social connections in the community they are "Indians" (Speck 1943:137). Family, tradition, society, genealogy, and history are far more cogent factors in determining one's status as Indian than is biology. Surnames are often indicators of an Indian background. Some of the more common names which are either exclusively Indian or tend to be Indian are: Billiot, Deon (Dion), Gregoire, Naquin, Parfait, and Verdin. An Indian can move away from his home area and "pass" as a White, or be mistaken for a Negro, but when he returns, he is an Indian (Roy 1959:89). Some intermarriage does occur but it is, as a rule, into the Negro group. This is usually by Indians who have suspected Negro ancestry and who are therefore not fully comfortable in the Indian community. The children of such a union are accepted into the Negro community and are not socially "Indians." If an Indian marries a White, the couple will generally leave the community and settle elsewhere.

The hospitals in the area no longer use the "Indian" category for their birth records. A child born of an Indian mother is now automatically classed as "White" on its birth certificate. Until recently, the option of racial designation was left to the judgment of the person who recorded the birth. As a result, individuals within a single family who are all recognized in the community as being Indians have birth certificates designating them as either White, Negro, or Indian—depending on when they were born and the judgment of the person who recorded the birth (Roy 1959).

Culturally, the Indians are quite close to the local Cajun French, for they have lost their traditional Indian culture and have adopted the rural Cajun French ways. Their religion, folklore, language, dwellings, surnames, and occupations are mostly Cajun. Even when Swanton visited these people in 1907, he could find little of cultural significance that connected them with their Indian past.

The most significant social group among the Houma is the extended family. An Indian identifies with his kindred and finds security and support in this association. Siblings, cousins, uncles, and aunts, all are central elements in an Indian's social life, and loyalty to the kin group is his primary social responsibility. Some find this situation to be a restriction on their private affairs and try to break out of it, but they usually return to it when they need help, especially in finances. There are few Indians who have become independent of their kin group. Those few who have succeeded have either turned their back on the Indian element in the community or left the area entirely.

It is difficult to be well-to-do and still maintain strong ties with kinsmen. Still, no man is expected to subsidize everyone in his extended family. A handful of men have been sufficiently generous to satisfy their kinship obligations and still be moderately successful in their personal financial affairs. These men are admired because they must be hard-working and thrifty in order to maintain such a balance. They are the unofficial spokesmen for the Indian community because non-Indians can appreciate their achievements and other Indians trust their judgment.

The general poverty level of the Indians has put them in a precarious position with the local non-Indian merchants and storekeepers. The seasonal and sporadic nature of employment of so many of these people forces them to buy on credit, and most families are deeply in debt to the local store. Any money that a person earns must be used to pay part of the debt owed to the merchant, for not to do so would risk the cancellation of credit privileges in the future. This is the familiar merchant-creditor relationship. Since so many Indians have hopelessly overdrawn accounts, the merchant has considerable influence in their affairs. He can exert strong pressures on those who are in debt to him. He also uses his influence to protect their economic welfare when it is to his long-term advantage, not because of a feeling of compassion, but for his own interests.

In the last decade much has changed in the Houma situation. All of the children now have access to schools, although the quality of education in some of the schools is questionable. Still, attempts are being made to improve education. The schools in the area are now fully integrated along geographic lines, thus putting Indian and Negro children in classrooms with White children. Various private and religious groups are working to provide recreation, skills improvement, and adequate health treatment for all underprivileged persons in the community, regardless of race or social background. Employment opportunities are more plentiful now than ever before. To be sure, many of the jobs offer low wages and require long hours of hard work, but work is available to those who want a job. Private ownership of small businesses and shrimping boats is now a reality to a few Indians; a generation ago it was only a distant hope.

## CULTURAL CHANGE

The Houma Indian situation offers an interesting case in the study of the movement from isolation into more and more integration with the larger society. This movement can be traced through three different stages, although the changes have been gradual, and, therefore, the chronological cut-off points are somewhat arbitrary.

The first stage can be termed social and geographical isolation, an extension of the earlier pattern of settlement developed by the Houma during their sojourn in Ascension Parish. The people lived as semi-nomadic hunters, trappers, and fishers, and drifted rather freely through the marsh and swamp country of southern Louisiana (Speck 1943:141). They were a self-contained community existing in relative isolation. The main reason for contact with the non-Indian community was for trade in order to get cloth, metal artifacts, and some foods which could not be produced locally. Otherwise, these people were self-sufficient and independent of the outside culture. This type of a community began to break up when professional trappers entered the area in the early part of the twentieth century. Further disturbance came with the establishment of fish and shrimp canneries which began to attract Indian laborers. The final blow came in the latter part of the 1920s, when the rich oil and natural gas fields were discovered in the area.

The second phase, social isolation, began as the Indians left their semi-nomadic hunting camps and settled in clusters at the termini of the roads which had been built into the swamp and marsh country. This clustering was the result of the establishment of the oil and gas fields in the area forcing the Indians to leave their isolated camps in the swamps and marshes. It was a gradual movement which began in the 1920s and continued until the late 1950s, and it was greatest just prior to and during the Second World War. In 1940, it was estimated that there were 700 Indians within walking distance of Dulac (Speck 1943:215), and by 1960, the movement into more accessible, permanent communities was complete.

In this second phase, the Indians came into casual contact with non-Indians, but these were of no great significance in their lives. Their home life and most intimate personal contacts were with other Indians. As general and unskilled laborers, the Indians worked in subordinate positions, having only limited contacts with their non-Indian employers and co-workers. Some religious groups did establish churches and schools in the Houma settlements, but these were attended exclusively by Indians (Fischer 1968:139). The parish made only feeble attempts to help Indian children obtain an education.

School attendance was difficult, and there was very little effort made by the parish school officials to enforce truancy laws against the absentee children. The Indian schools were substandard and under-financed, and during this period very few Indians received an adequate education (Fischer 1968: 140-41).

The pressures of the Second World War and the great industrial, technical, and economic "boom" which followed finally brought the Indians into the third and present stage of a closer association with the rest of the nation. Increasing petrochemical operations, both on land and in the Gulf of Mexico, have resulted in the establishment of supply depots and satellite companies to support their needs. The commercial fishing fleet has greatly expanded; the existing fish canneries have enlarged and new ones have been established. There has been a significant influx of Whites and some Negroes into the area to work and operate these new facilities and to open busi-nesses to serve the growing population. However, good land for settlement and commercial use is still severely limited because of the swampy nature of the area, and all six of the communities concerned in this study stretch out in line settlement fashion along the bayous. The Dulac-Grand Caillou community is over eight miles long but extends only a few hundred yards wide on either side of the bayou, and newcomers have built their homes where space could be found. This has resulted in a generally desegregated situation, although there have been more than a few cases in which Indians lost title and deed or rights to use their land and have been forced to settle elsewhere.

With the expansion and growth in these communities Indian life has changed considerably, and the Indians are now a minority in all but one community. Even in Dulac, their largest settlement, there are twice as many Whites as Indians. Many of the new arrivals are from outside Louisiana and even from outside the South. The French language and customs are no longer a general part of the total cultural milieu, and the institutions of the Houma Indians have become integrated into a larger whole. Schooling is available to those who want it. There has been a change in the legal system in which Indians are beginning to have faith in the protection of their rights. An intensive voter registration drive has finally given them some small measure of political influence. Improved literacy, health, and transportation have opened new job opportunities. Some Indians now own small businesses and commercial fishing craft, and Indian youth can now pass the minimum physical and mental qualifications of the armed forces, which enables them to turn to the military for vocational training.

### THE FUTURE OF THE HOUMA

The Houma Indians are now a part of the greater cultural community of southern Louisiana and of the nation. Circumstances and events have made a return to their former free-roving, semi-nomadic life impossible. The current trend seems to indicate an even greater association with the non-Indian community and a steady decline of the traditional Indian norms and values.

A vital question generated by the rapidly changing situation concerns the effect of such change on group cohesiveness. Kinship ties and the French language still bind the Houma together as a group distinct from their non-Indian neighbors (Fischer 1968:147; Parenton and Pellegrin 1950:152). Nowadays, however, the individual finds increasing pressures from outside the Indian community which make him less dependent on his kindred and more attracted to non-Indian lifeways. Schools, the military, outmigration, the automobile, television, Protestant missionaries, community centers, better jobs, integrated neighborhoods, fluency in English, and other related factors have all had their role in breaking down the traditional Houma society. The individuals who have readily accepted the changing conditions often find themselves at variance with others who would wish to maintain a more traditional orientation. The close social bond of the Indian community is not so significant to one who can successfully function in the context of the greater, non-Indian community. The material improvements of the mid-twentieth century have, therefore, made the individual less dependent upon the group. Some who can leave the area because of acquired skills do, and as such are no longer primary members of the local community. Many emigrés contribute to the support of their kinsmen who remain in the Indian community, enabling even more individuals to gain the skills and ability to leave, especially if they are young. Most of those who leave go to urban areas.

By the late nineteen-sixties, this rural to urban migration was well under way with a predictable increase in intensity as more and more people found that they could function in a non-Indian world. This type of process will tend to leave the older and more conservative individuals behind as a majority within the Houma community.

Most Houma would prefer to remain among their friends and relatives, but there are not enough jobs to support them. The future does not offer an easy solution to the problems raised by rapid cultural change. What it does offer is a chance to feel a sense of individual worth and dignity, and to be free from poverty, ignorance, and debt.

The question may now be asked as to what the over-all and lasting consequences of such a change to the Houma Indian community will be. Will the group continue to be socially identifiable with its close kinship ties and basic Cajun French culture? Or, will it gradually fade into the larger "mega-culture" of America? These questions must wait to be fully answered by the passage of time.

## NOTES

1. The background data for this study were gathered by the researcher at Louisiana State University. The actual field research was conducted during a six-week period in the summer of 1969. The project was funded through a National Science Foundation Summer Traineeship. The researcher lived in the Dulac Community Center, which is supported by the United Methodist Church, and he gathered the data in the capacity of a community worker. No attempt was made to conceal the fact that the researcher was an anthropologist involved in a community study, but the local residents thought of him and accepted him as a community worker. The Center and its workers are accepted and respected by the local people, and this enabled the researcher to make meaningful contacts.

2. The term "Cajun" is a corruption of the French pronunciation of the word "Acadien." It is freely used by both the French-speaking and English-speaking people in the area and does not have a negative or derogatory connotation.

3. John Swanton visited these people in 1907 (Fischer 1968:6) in an official capacity for the federal government and reported that they were not "pure" enough to qualify for federal help. His visit was brief and his conclusions are debatable. Still, as a result of his recommendations, the Houma were not given any recognition by the government.

4. These settlements, from west to east are: DuLarge, along Bayou DuLarge; Dulac, along Bayou Grand Caillou and Bayou Dulac; Pointe au Barree (Lower Montegut), along Bayou Terrebonne; Lower Pointe au Chien, along Bayou Pointe au Chien; Champs Charles (Isle St. Jean Charles), along Bayou St. Jean Charles; and, Lower Bayou Lafourche, along Bayou Lafourche (in both Terrebonne and Lafourche parishes).

## REFERENCES

Fischer, Ann, 1968. History and Current Status of the Houma Indians. In *The American Indian Today*, Stuart Levine and Nancy O. Lurie, eds. (Deland, Florida: Everett/Edwards).

Parenton, Vernon J. and Roland J. Pellegrin, 1950. The Sabines. *Social Forces* 29:148-154.

Roy, Edison Peter, 1959. *The Indians of Dulac*, unpublished master's thesis (Baton Rouge: Louisiana State University).

Speck, Frank G., 1943. A Social Reconnaissance of the Creole Houma
    Indian Trappers of the Louisiana Bayous. *American Indigena*
    3:134-146, 212-220.
Swanton, John R., 1911. Indian Tribes of the Lower Mississippi River
    and the Adjacent Coast of the Gulf of Mexico. *Bulletin of the
    Bureau of American Ethnology*, no. 43.
——————————, 1946. The Indians of the Southeastern United States.
    *Bulletin of the Bureau of American Ethnology*, no. 137.
United States Department of Commerce, Bureau of the Census, 1963.
    United States Census of Population: 1960. *Characteristics of the
    Population*, vol. 1, part 20, Louisiana.

# Potters in a Changing South

ROBERT SAYERS

THE general character of the South today might best be conveyed in a single theme: "A region in transition."[1] One need only look to the large store of current literature concerned with developments in the economic and technological spheres, urbanization, and the Civil Rights movement to draw truth from this statement. And yet, for all of this emphasis on broad regional modification, we still find a considerable number of instances on the local level where change is only grudgingly acknowledged. Indeed, certain institutions or traditions which appear to have passed from the scene without fanfare elsewhere have managed in many quarters of the South to hold their own, even in the face of growing obsolescence. This "conservative bent" became particularly evident to me when in 1968 I visited and interviewed at length numbers of Southern hand-craftsmen who were caught between the times but were trying to shore up rather than abandon their faltering trade. Because I see in this response much to suggest a regional phenomenon inextricably tied in with the area's history and sociocultural organization, I should like to say more about these artisans and their craft.

Pottery manufacture has long been an important domestic hand-craft industry in the Southern states, even after the trade faltered elsewhere. In 1940, Helen Stiles accounted for some 200 working potters in North Carolina alone (1941:166); and similar numbers probably were to be found elsewhere in the region at that time. Today "old-time" potters are still plentiful, though perhaps not quite so numerous. What is interesting to note, however, is that the widespread proliferation of glass and tin containers into all but the most isolated of Southern communities shortly after the turn of the present century should have spelled the end of the rural ceramist's art. But, as I have just implied, it did not.

Before I attempt to explain why potters still abound in the

region, I would first like to present brief sketches of two families of present-day Southern potters, the Meaders and the Browns. Hopefully, from these sketches some of the important elements of the craft tradition will become obvious. The following features are noteworthy: each family's efforts to maintain the institution; accommodations to changing markets, technologies, and the physical environment; and finally, similarities and differences between the two families.

THE MEADERS POTTERY

The town of Cleveland sits in a piedmont area just south of the Smoky Mountains in northern Georgia. A rural hamlet until early in the century, Cleveland is situated at the top of the cotton belt and was once a center for north Georgian pottery manufacture. Cleveland now appears headed on a downhill drift. Young forests cover the surrounding countryside revealing here and there a reminder of the cotton era. Kudzu (*Pueraria thunbergiana*), a vine introduced in the 1940s to check erosion, has largely taken over whole sections of the land adding to the forbidding "feel" of the outlying region where few people still live, I was told, "because of a lowered water table."

Cleveland itself with its courthouse, town square, historical society, and various small businesses, is much like any other settlement in that part of the state. Religious activity, where it is apparent, is of the fundamentalist sort, characterized by large evening revivals. Unemployment is widespread, and I saw few young people. Attempts on the part of the city chamber of commerce to attract a tourist trade seem to be less successful than similar attempts made by nearby Dahlonega.

Today the only working potteries in Cleveland are the Cheever Meaders Pottery and the Robert Owens Pottery, the latter developed and run by a young college instructor and consequently of little concern here. The former establishment, on the other hand, has been standing in its present location south of town since 1887. Rich in pottery lore, the shop is one of many with the Meaders name that have dotted north Georgia since 1830 or before, the first member of the clan having migrated to nearby Banks County from Virginia about that time (Ramsay 1939:237).

The Meaders, however, were not the only potter family in the region. Through the late 1920s, many other working potteries were to be found scattered throughout White, Hall, and Banks Counties. Early in the present century there were at least eight individual shops in Cleveland alone, two belonging to Meaders boys and the others belonging to Dorseys and Pitchfords. Of all of these north Georgia potteries perhaps three remain.

It was in this section of the country that potters took to the open road as "wagoners," often peddling their produce as far distant as North Carolina before returning home. Most of these men farmed or tended livestock in their spare hours away from the pottery. Families ranged on the large side, as is common in nearly all rural communities.

Common tools of the Georgian trade included mule-drawn pug-mills, hand-cranked glaze-mills (these look like a millstone set into a flat-horizontal slab), treadle kick wheels, outdoor tunnel kilns, and row upon row of large stoneware churns, crocks, pitchers, and jugs. These vessels were glazed with flint, feldspar, iron-sand, and sand-and-ash glazes as well as with the conventional Albany Slip, the latter probably introduced into the region at some point after 1890. It is unlikely that any of the ware was ever stamped.

By the time of the Great Depression, a decline in the region and the degeneration of the cotton trade had forced most of the potters out of business. Only the Meaders Pottery along with a handful of others survived. Interestingly enough, Cheever Meader's son, Lanier, sees the Depression as a time of productivity rather than decline for his "daddy":

> People at that time was all out of work and didn't have anything to eat and nowhere to go. And this business here—my dad was making churns. That's all he ever liked to make anyhow. For some reason—I can't understand it—he really had a heyday with it: five to ten cents per gallon (and now it's seventy-five cents). People used more of our ware then and somehow they managed to find a nickel or a dime or a quarter to buy a four-or-five gallon churn. If anybody didn't have a job, they'd have a garden. And if they didn't grow it, they didn't eat. If they didn't *preserve* it after they growed it, they didn't have it to eat then. And that's the reason, I reckon, the churns sold so well. And we didn't go hungry either!

Up until this point all of the Meaders males had made a career of pottery-turning. However, following the hard times, only Cheever and Lanier continued the family operation. Two of Lanier's brothers found work in a lumber yard and a poultry farm respectively, a third learning the electrician's trade. Even Lanier himself occasionally took time off from the pottery to seek work in a local metalshop and in surrounding textile mills. Asked whether his father intended

that he become a potter, Lanier replied: "Well, I wouldn't say that
for not knowing. It's more circumstance than anything else." This
answer is probably a considerable understatement in light of what
we shall see later.

In 1952 Lanier Meaders built a new shop for his father to replace
the older building, which was in a state of disrepair. He also continued working at a local metalworks and tended the farm. Upon
Cheever Meader's death in 1967, Lanier returned full-time to the
family industry. Today, at age 53 and still single, he turns ware at
the pottery alongside his mother. Sometimes he has only to work but
two or three hours a day. Because there is virtually no competition
for his kind of ware and because he is a skilled artisan, Cheever's son
is able to do amazingly well for himself.

Minor changes in the shop in the past two years have included
a new oil kiln and a small mechanical clay grinder which Lanier de-
vised and built himself from scraps he brought home from the metalshop. The mule is gone but the old pugmill remains. The glaze-mill
also stands as usual but is seldom used. Lanier is hesitant to dispose of it,
although at least one state museum is interested.

Clay is difficult to obtain these days even though a rich deposit
sits within a few hundred yards of the pottery shed. The proprietor of
the land it rests on would probably be willing to let the Meaders
mine the pit in return for rent except that another man has a lien
on the land and will not let the "owner" use any of its resources.
Such a situation is not uncommon around Cleveland.

Another feature of the Meaders Pottery that has not changed
appreciably over the years is the product. Lanier still turns large,
heavy churns as did his father and his father before that. In addition,
he makes an occasional "face" jug, part of a long tradition in
Southern pottery-making. His mother has been turning ornamental
pieces such as bird-houses and decorative vases since around 1950,
but Lanier does not consider these things "old-time" or traditional—
much the same reaction he displays toward Bob Owen's ware.

Customers who patronize the Meaders Pottery are mostly local
residents who buy churns in which to pickle beans and sauerkraut
and to store meat, both common activities in rural areas of the South.
Glass bottles and tin cans are readily available these days, but Lanier's
stoneware "churns" do the trick more efficiently, as they always have.
Mr. Meaders also attracts a great many tourists and a small group
of folk art collectors, but he appears bothered by these, especially
the former.

Asked to characterize his life as a potter, Lanier Meaders has these words:

> Well, it's just a trade. It's a gift that a person comes by. I could no more stop this than I could fly an airplane. All my movements, all of my work that I've done all my life has led one way or another straight to this place right here and every time I come about it, I'm just a little bit deeper into it. If a man's really farming, he's got a job every day, rain or shine. But if he don't farm no more than I do—no more than he has to—then this pottery makes everything balance out. This is quick money. I used to think that it was hard, but it's not. It's easy work.

## THE BROWN POTTERY

Arden, North Carolina, unlike Cleveland, lies in close proximity to a small urban center. Stretched out along State Highway 25 traveling in a southbound direction from Asheville, the town is predominantly an area of light industry (paper mills) with some small businesses and a remnant of a former farming economy. Several trucking concerns, machine shops, and dragstrips are nearby, and most of the men in Arden are skilled auto mechanics. The Asheville Airport, a half-mile distant, also affords some employment opportunities. By and large, Arden seems to be a modest, low-middle income community in transition from a traditional rural economy to a semi-industrial one, even though the nearness of Asheville has probably always lent the town some familiarity with urban ways.

Those persons whom I met in Arden were generally conservative, religious (though not fundamentalist), and showed an interest in other regions beyond their own, many of the men having served overseas duty during the World War or having vacationed up North. Teenagers around Arden are fond of cars, often joining together in informal auto clubs. Few Blacks were encountered, although a great many live in Asheville. The Cherokee Indian Reservation is just to the west, and occasionally Indians come down to the pottery for trade but have little other interest in the town.

Three Brown potteries stand in and around the local area today. Of these, the oldest (and the one I shall speak the most about) is the Davis Brown Pottery just off to one side of Highway 25. Originally founded in 1923 by Davis and his brother, Javan Brown, it was maintained by the former until his death in 1967. Now Davis' son, Louis Brown, operates the pottery with his family. Javan Brown, on the other hand, is still alive at age 72 and has his own shop in

Valdes. His son, Evan Javan Brown, Jr., runs the third shop, Evan's Pottery, in nearby Skyland.

One more pottery, and perhaps the original establishment in the region, belonged to a Mr. Stevens who died some years ago at an advanced age. Steven's Pottery now belongs to a pair of young men who have renamed it the "Pisgah Forest Pottery." Like Bob Owens, these men did not grow up in the potter families (which I shall henceforth refer to as "dynasties").

Like the Meaders, the Browns were settled in various parts of the South by 1830. The first Brown potter in the United States seems to have been an English immigrant tradesman named John Henry Brown. Whether this man settled immediately in the South or not is unknown. However, by the time he fathered a son, he was living in South Carolina. The present Brown potters in Arden, Louis Brown and his sons, represent the sixth and seventh generations of ceramists in direct line from this man.

At the time the Arden pottery was built, conditions remained much the same as those described for the Meaders pottery. As in Cleveland, part of the year the men would take to the road as wagoners, peddling their stoneware to merchants in not-too-distant communities. On occasion such trips were not necessary, for a trader would come by the shop and buy all the ware the potters had stock-piled, but this did not happen too often. When Davis and Javan Brown's brothers would travel up to the shop from Georgia (some worked at potteries around Atlanta; others worked in and around Cleveland), the men divided their time between the pottery and a baseball team that would play all comers from the local textile mills.

As the Great Depression swept through the South, the brothers scattered, leaving again only Davis and Javan, the original founders. (Unlike the Meaders, none of the Brown boys gave up the craft at this point; they simply moved elsewhere, often hiring out as pottery-turners in other men's shops). When Javan Brown, too, left for a time to build kilns for artisans elsewhere, the remaining Brown potter was left much to his own devices. Here the Browns diverge from the Meaders, for Davis Brown sought to restructure his formerly traditional industry.

Before the nation found itself involved in another world war, Davis had remodeled his machinery and introduced to his pottery the new manufacturing techniques of jiggering and slip-casting. He even renovated the large wood-burning kiln so that it would fire coal, since good pine wood was becoming scarce. In 1939 the original Brown Pottery was torn down and a larger, more efficient building constructed to house both the machines and the kilns.

The most important contribution that Davis Brown made in "modernizing" the pottery, however, was in terms of the product. He began production of a new line of ware to be sold directly to department stores in the large cities—coffee cups, mugs, flower pots, vases, ash trays, pie plates, tea pots, cups and saucers, and any custom item which might be in demand. Each piece bore the stamp: BROWN POTTERY. ARDEN, N. C. In addition, Davis systematized his ware into categories, listing some 120 different shapes and sizes.

Early during World War II, Mr. Brown also began experimenting with a French style of cooking ware dubbed "Valorware." Created after painstaking trials with local clays, the new casseroles readily found a market through a New York distributor who could no longer import similar ceramics from overseas. By 1942 Davis had as many as twenty-six persons working for him making Valorware at the shop in Arden. But the boom did not last.

After Japan surrendered, laborers in the pottery, who had found plenty of work during tough times, began drifting away. Innovations came more slowly, even with the shift from coal to oil and, ultimately, to gasoline fuel in the big kiln. Davis's own two sons, Louis and Edward, like the rest (and like Cheever Meader's boys following the Depression) began to take an interest in other endeavors. Louis had served in the Armed Forces during the War and was now working on diesel engines, formally learning the trade in Chicago. Returning to Arden sometime in the late 1940s, he put this knowledge of mechanics to practical use by accepting a job with a local trucking firm where he remains employed to this day.

However, with his father's death in 1967, Louis Brown fell heir to the family pottery. Because his seven-day-a-week job at the trucking plant cuts into so much of his time, his nearly-grown boys, Charles and Robert, have been left with most of the daytime chores around the shop. They turn out orders as they come in and prepare demonstrations for the daily busloads of tourists who pass through to see the well-known Brown Pottery, home of the "original" Little Brown Jug. As such, the family manages to attract a modest tourist and mail order market for their heavy patent-glazed ware. Little about the shop has changed since World War II. Even the building is something of an anachronism, surrounded as it is by numerous filling stations, motels, taverns, and small businesses.

Nevertheless, Louis Brown has plans for the shop "when it'll be possible to give more time to it." He reads ceramic trade journals and makes minor alterations here and there such as replacing the old glaze buckets with marshmallow topping containers for the benefit of their teflon linings. Looking toward the future, Mr. Brown has the following to say:

> In my opinion the shop can be improved and updated. I like to see modern things and I like to see old-time things, and in the pottery business you can see both. If a machine nowadays will do the job better, I believe in using that machine. We still have the old kickwheel here [actually a treadle-type wheel]. I think the kick-wheel is fine, but I'd hate to know that I had to make 500 gallons of churns a day on the kickwheel like those old-timers used to have to do. We don't really have that type of work to do and it would be unnecessary if you did it nowadays that way, because they've got power wheels and better machinery. We should use those new inventions as time goes on to keep intact [sic] with time and keep production up with the demand.
>
> I don't think the craft and the potter's wheel and the potter is going to go completely out, although in our lives and the generations behind us there's not been near as many potters as other skilled trades, because it takes so long to learn. That's why I think it helps in a long period of time to get potters encouraged to keep changing.

### THE SOUTHERN POTTERY TRADITION

From these two thumbnail sketches, we can see that change has taken place to varying degrees and with varying results in both instances over the past 70 years. But where do the two families converge? Is there any basic similarity between the Meaders and the Browns beyond the fact that they share the same trade? Here I believe it would do well to look to the region's past.

Several important factors affected the course of Southern history in a fashion unlike that in other parts of the country. Predominantly a producer of a few plant staples and allied products—cotton and tobacco, textiles and petrochemicals—the South on the whole proved mainly a builder of small, isolated communities rather than large-scale cities (Reissman 1965:80). In addition, these communities were relatively static—almost homogeneous in ethnic and religious background (at least for whites) and uncontaminated by alien influxes from the outside, both in terms of human immigration and in terms of "culture capital" flow, that is, knowledge. Indeed, what movement there was seemed to proceed in the opposite direction, ". . . including [emigrants] who might have questioned or challenged the [standing] traditions" (Reissman 1965:81).

And yet there is a third element in the South's past that has the most bearing on contemporary potters. Colonial historian Carl Bridenbaugh notes the unusual dearth of middle class craftsmen in the lower colonies during the formative stages of "regionalization" ". . . whose skills and solid worth as citizens would have contributed greatly to the common weal" (1950:32). Instead, it appears that skilled handcraft labor was virtually non-existent in the area at a time when, by comparison, craftsmen comprised close to eighteen percent of the general population in the settled colonies of the North, next only in numbers to husbandmen (Bridenbaugh n.d.:1). There are several reasons behind this interesting phenomenon.

In the first place, many successful Northern craft industries were initiated by immigrant tradesmen or others newly apprenticed on these shores. Clustering around moderately large communities, these men enjoyed a prosperous business and a respectable status as suppliers of the everyday items common to nearly all households. Even though the domestic product rarely equalled in quality that made overseas, it found favor with a sizable portion of the populace who deemed it troublesome, expensive, or unpatriotic (during the American Revolution) to import all their ware. Therefore, the crafts provided a livelihood for large numbers of colonists who did not farm.

By contrast, the South attracted few experienced artisans from outside until a late date. The isolated, primitive complexion of Southern settlements, the limited amount of capital resources, and the disinterest of the landed gentry in locally-made ware—all of these factors discouraged the formation of an immigrant middle class (Ramsay 1939:28).

Southern society militated as well against the spontaneous growth of its own indigenous body of skilled craftsmen. Patrons, who occasionally subsidized artisans in the North, were unknown, even in cities like Charleston and Atlanta. Apprenticeships too were seldom to be had except by orphans and other unfortunates who were simply bound over to a trade until maturity for the sake of convenience (Bridenbaugh 1950:30-31).

Moreover, as land holdings in the region began to increase, Black labor was imported in large numbers. Rather than serve as field-hands, many Negroes in the pre-Revolutionary period learned semi-skilled crafts and turned out crude ware for local consumption (Bridenbaugh 1950:15). Therefore, of those white artisans who were attracted to the South at this early date, few remained craftsmen for very long. Cheap land and social standing usually meant more than the prospect of competing with Blacks.

To be sure, white hand-craftsmen, including potters, were established in the South after the middle 1700s (probably because utilitarian ware had to be made and could not always be imported or manufactured by slaves), but these men had neither the skill nor the status of their Northern counterparts. Rather, it is more likely that they were typical of some of the "low-lifes" of the region. Potters throughout north Georgia today remark, though mostly in jest, that their forebears likely were refugees from some British debtor's prison.

By the time of the Civil War, potters who were not conscripted into the Confederate Army did their share for the war effort by turning medicine jars, mugs, bowls, and chamber pots for the Southern hospitals (Spargo 1948:96). After the conflict, the number of small establishments increased markedly throughout the entire region, since outside sources for ceramics were largely closed off. A unique feature of the Southern craft at this time was the emergence of countless "jugtowns" in response to the demand from local distilleries for liquor containers, a demand which continued unabated until Prohibition. From this period down through the earlier part of this century, the same isolation and independence of foreign innovation and idea that had characterized the Southern potteries for nearly 200 years still prevailed.

Taking all of these historical features into consideration then, we might suggest that Southern potteries formed institutionalized identities peculiar to their own region from a very early time— traditions which, when reinforced over several generations, would prove exceedingly difficult to alter or abandon as future conditions and events demanded. And so saying, I wish to return now to the two families of potters as a means for illustrating those structural features which can be said to underlie a "Southern Pottery Tradition." Each category has a basis in historical fact, although some are more important to the maintenance of the industry than are others, and some are no longer applicable (as noted). However, I think all are important to an understanding of the change situation.

1. Male potters. Without exception, men have always been the pottery-turners in the South, although their wives often help around the shop. And though a woman might try her hand on the wheel (like Lanier Meaders's mother), she will never be considered a genuine potter. Interestingly enough, this situation frees the females in potter families from the "dynasty" while the men remain bound, as we shall see presently.

2. A low social position. In neither Arden nor Cleveland could I determine that members of potter families were ever ascribed a status lower than that of their non-ceramist neighbors. Therefore, I would assume that this trait—if, indeed, it ever existed as Bridenbaugh suggests—had disappeared before the time of those craftsmen and family members with whom I talked. Perhaps it was the demise of the plantation system after the Civil War and the subsequent dimming of distinctions between planter, merchant, sharecropper, artisan, slave, and so on that brought about this change.

3. A lack of formal training. Genuine apprenticeships have been the exception to the rule in the South, since most technical learning occurred in the home. Many potters like Javan Brown spent time working for other concerns besides the family shop, but they usually learned the basic skills of the trade from their fathers beginning at a very early age. Also this training was more the "learn as you go along" variety than it was the "do as I do" sort, if my observations are correct. I asked both Louis Brown and his sons at separate times about firing the big gas kiln. Their answers differed markedly as to what happens—even down to the procedure for bricking up the door —and this in spite of the fact that the older boy, Charles, has been working in the pottery for almost fifteen years.

4. Isolated shops with local markets. Through the early part of this century, all potters turned ware for the local community (excepting those instances already mentioned). On the other point, however, one might question whether or not the shops were truly isolated from one another in view of the many potteries in and around Cleveland, Georgia. And yet it seems that the craftsmen—even brothers—rarely interacted, preferring to remain fairly close to their own shops most of the time. This peculiar behavior might relate to competition for customers as Louis Brown supposes: "I don't think that any potters ever stuck together. If they had, they would have cut one another's throats with prices." Rivalry and trade secrecy might enter the picture as well.

Another possible reason for this anti-social posture would be simply that the potter was too busy to socialize. It is significant that George Foster, speaking about Mexican peasant artisans, should offer: "In my experience, it is the rare potter who, without unusual stimulus, is much interested in how other potters work or what they make (1965:55)." Even today the point may be well taken as regards Southern potters. Louis Brown, when driving me to the Pisgah Forest Pottery some few miles distant from Arden for an interview, mentioned that he had not been out that way for years.

Even more improbable, while Louis and his uncle, Javan, have always known of the Meaders Pottery a hundred miles to the south-west (Javan having even worked there), no one has been down to Cleveland for at least three decades. Nor have the Meaders placed any calls with the Browns in all that time.

5. A utilitarian product. All ware turned prior to this century (with the exception of that made for the Confederacy during the War Between the States) was made for local use and consisted of those same kinds of articles that Lanier Meaders still favors: churns, crocks, pitchers, jugs (including "face" jugs), and so forth. Later we see the development of trade with local distilleries and, still later, a tourist orientation.

6. Dynastic regeneration. This is certainly the most important feature of the Southern craft, and for nearly 200 years has contributed to the continued maintenance of artisans in a region basically hostile or indifferent to their presence. And it is this aspect of the Southern pottery tradition that is presently making it exceedingly difficult for young members of potter families to break with the craft altogether, even in the face of its increasing obsolescence.

What the process means, ultimately, is that *all* sons of potters were trained from a very early age to continue the family craft when their father died—in other words, "like father, like son." Until quite a late time, this was the rule. However, the young man's fate was usually accepted, since in the rural South of some forty or fifty years ago, he had few other alternatives besides farming. Besides that, potters still speak of an intangible: "Pottery gets to you!" And anyone to whom pottery had "got" at the age of five or six was probably pretty well stuck until more glamorous occupations coupled with a decline in the craft's utility came along. And even then it might prove difficult to turn one's back upon six generations of forebears.

## Change in the Tradition

Just as the process of dynastic regeneration served to accommodate the region's need for artisans whom it could not attract from elsewhere, it did one other thing: it chained these same craftsmen to a trade that was gradually losing its usefulness. Held captive to a limited and poorly-championed technology, a slow inflow of new ideas, a local market which demanded a specific utilitarian ware for home use, and a unique social and cultural tradition that placed severe limits on male members of the family, the craft was slowly strangling in the wake of industrialization. However, it was only when clay products began to give way to glass bottles and tin cans and when this trend was taken in combination with the development of new employment opportunities in the local community that we see potters quitting (as in Cleveland). Probably even this was not enough—it took a catastrophic event like the Great Depression or World War II to convince many younger potters that their place was no longer in the work shed.

A second response to a changing economic milieu, and perhaps more common than that just described, was an attempt to alter either one's product or one's market orientation—or both. Most of the older, established potters did this, some faring better than others. Davis Brown, combining genuine innovative abilities with foresight and a fortuitous location for his pottery, was the most spectacularly successful of these. The rest, like Cheever Meaders (and now Lanier) made little concession to change but sold their ware to tourist and neighbor alike for as long as they were able.

But what of the future? That some persons seem determined to further the tradition is fairly clear. One son of each of the older potters (Cheever Meaders's son, Lanier; Davis Brown's son, Louis; and Javan Brown's son, Evan) is doing what he can to preserve the craft. This suggests that the dynasty is breaking up in its original form, but that it is continuing to insure each family pottery's survival for a while. That both Louis Brown and his cousin Evan hold second jobs, however, is going to make a difference. Nevertheless both men are training their children as potters—Louis has his two sons who work alongside him in the shop; and Evan, having no sons, has sent his daughter to college to learn ceramics. It seems likely that these individuals will have a greater right to self-determination than did their fathers and grandfathers when it comes to choosing an occupation.

Assuming that a seventh generation of Brown potters does find its place at the wheel (and I believe this will occur), we can look for still further divergence from the traditional norm to compensate for ever-increasing social and economic change in the region. As I see it, aside from the large, industrialized manufacturer of ceramic tableware (who does not concern us here), tomorrow's potter in the South will have to depend even less upon the once-stable market for general household goods (cooking and storage vessels, decorative vases, lamp bases, etc.) than at present and more upon specialized ware (unglazed garden pottery) and novelty items (tourist knick-knacks). The former of these two alternatives is still fairly secure; the latter much less so though perhaps catering to a more visible and attractive market initially. Nevertheless, there are just so many tourists, and the better potter is the only one who will be able to earn a living day in and day out. Therefore, family tradition will no longer be enough to hold the craftsman to the task and Southern institutions will no longer demand that the region produce potters. Skill, creativity, and competitive spirit will better characterize the survivor, much the situation that remains for the small businessman or artisan elsewhere in the United States.

### CONCLUSIONS

It is implicit in my introduction that the South, until recent times, has undergone a unique historical experience quite apart from the mainstream of industrial American life and that the consequences of this distinct regional "imprint" have often been a slowness to innovate and an overall tendency toward conservatism. Even by 1940, "the South [when compared with the national average] consistently showed a lower level of economic productivity, and a lower proportion of people living in the cities" (Reissman 1965:81). I have here attempted to demonstrate how the structuring of a particular institution when combined with a long period of social and cultural stability (those centuries of Southern experience prior to the advent of industrialization) might hinder any such forces of change once they are introduced into a region.

This point assumes particular importance when we begin to compare other formerly stable, agrarian societies only now beginning to experience urbanization and industrialization with the situation just described for the South. It is my hope that someone might find useful a modified folk society model (after Foster's [1953] "folk culture" configuration) to describe and predict what happens when industrialization displaces a rural system with the pre-industrial city as a focal point. Because this is occurring among peasant and other pastoral peoples throughout the world, the problem should have more than academic interest.

### NOTES

1. Field work was undertaken in 1968 while I was a summer intern at the Smithsonian Institution and was directed by Mr. Ralph Rinzler, Division of Performing Arts, and Dr. Sam Stanley, Division of Anthropology. Financial assistance was provided by the National Science Foundation.

# REFERENCES

Bridenbaugh, Carl, 1950. *The Colonial Craftsmen* (New York: New York University Press, Washington Square).

------------------------- n.d. *Myths and Realities, Societies of the Colonial South* (New York: Atheneum).

Foster, George M., 1953. What is Folk Culture? *American Anthropologist* 55:159-173.

-------------------------, 1965. The Sociology of Pottery: Questions and Hypotheses Arising from Contemporary Mexican Work. In *Ceramics and Man*, F. R. Matson, ed. (Viking Fund Publications in Anthropology no. 41).

Ramsay, John, 1939. *American Potters and Pottery* (Hale, Cushman, and Flint).

Reissman, Leonard, 1965. Urbanization in the South. In *The South in Continuity and Change*, John C. McKinney and Edgar T. Thompson, eds. (Durham, North Carolina: Duke University Press).

Spargo, John, 1948. *Early American Pottery and China* (Garden City, New York: Garden City Publishing Co., Inc.).

Stiles, Helen E., 1941. *Pottery in the United States* (New York: E. P. Dutton and Co., Inc.).

# The Southern Protestant Ethic Disease

James L. Peacock

I would like to report some ideas about Southern religion and Southern mental illness that underlie an exploration I have begun at the state mental hospital at Butner, North Carolina.[1] The mental and cultural complex that I am investigating may be called the Southern Protestant Ethic Disease. The Southern Protestant Ethic Disease differs profoundly from the Classical Protestant Ethic Disease, which is probably better understood by psychiatrists.

Some of the differences between the two diseases should emerge from the following brief sketch, which is preliminary to the more disciplined research planned for Butner. What I have to say is based partly on exploratory interviews and mainly on deductions from premises underlying the Classical Protestant Ethic as defined by Max Weber (1968) and the Southern Protestant Ethic as defined by Samuel Hill (1966). The aim is to deduce the kinds of mental trouble and torment that are likely to come from the Southern as opposed to the Classical Protestant Ethic.

According to Weber, the Protestant Ethic derived from the Calvinistic belief in a terrifying distance between God and man. So distant was God that His will was unknowable to man in any determinate fashion. God had willed that some men be among the saved, others among the damned, but no man could learn definitely into which group he fell. None of the techniques or media of the medieval Church, such as rites or sacraments, could signal or assure a man's salvation. Seeking desperately to discover some sign or assurance, the Calvinist finally concluded that incessantly, methodically, and piously behaving *as if* he were called by God was the surest sign and assurance that he was in fact called by God to serve Him as one of the saved, the Elect.

The search for salvation thus drove the Calvinist Protestant to systematize his entire life into an incessant, methodical, pious, straight and narrow movement serving God's glory and kingdom. Waste of time was the deadliest of sins, since it distracted from this service. Regular and planned work was most desirable. Irregular or casual work was at best a necessary evil. Theater, idle talk, sex, adornment, or elaborate ceremony and ritual were sensuous and sinful distractions from the ascetic and disciplined life of service that thrust toward salvation.

The Southern Protestant faced the same problem: how to assure himself of salvation. The horrors of damnation loomed as vividly to him as to the Calvinist. His solution was, however, different. Instead of idealizing a total life of relentless, systematized, and cumulative service, the Southerner pinned his hopes almost entirely on a single instant of emotional, climactic, conversion experience. This instant need bear no integral relationship to the convert's total life plan, as is illustrated by an anecdote reported by Hill (1966:105). A Sunday school teacher, upon being asked by his pupil if Adolf Hitler was in heaven, replied that it was quite possible that at some point in his childhood Hitler had undergone the necessary conversion experience. The example is extreme, but it serves to illustrate that the Southern Protestant Ethic emphasizes the instantaneous conversion experience rather than the Classical Protestant Ethic of a life-long harnessing of self to God's plan.

Both the Southern and the Classical Protestant Ethic are ascetic. Both call for harsh discipline of body and senses. But the Classical Protestant Ethic defines such asceticism as a rational means toward more efficient service to God's ends. Lacking this orientation, the Southern Protestant Ethic views ascetic prohibitions less as efficient means toward ends than as absolute and unquestioned laws unto themselves. Taboos against drink, sex, and gambling acquire the character of primitive taboos.

The Classical Protestant has felt compelled to ruthlessly systematize more and more of life as service toward God's glory or some secular equivalent thereof: the great Anglo-American system of what Weber called "ascetic and bureaucratic capitalism" and, more recently, the Anglo-American welfare state are products of this compulsion (Peacock and Kirsch 1970: Chap. 6). The parallel compulsion of the Southerner has been to harshly discipline his impulses. Drink, sex, and the other joys have been the Southern Protestant's concern more than sloth, inefficiency, and human messiness that prompt the reforms of Classical Protestantism.

In addition to personal ethics, the Southerner has emphasized an interpersonal ethic whereby the personally righteous and admirable man stands as a model for others to emulate if they like (note the role of men like Robert E. Lee). This personable and voluntaristic ethic contrasts with the more distant and coercive one of Classical Protestantism. Classical Protestants move toward abstract schemes and plans that attack and reform unwilling and distant targets.

Given that a mental patient is strongly oriented in the Southern Protestant Ethic, how might his tensions, anxieties, frustrations, and symptoms differ from those of the Classical Protestant patient? The difference perhaps lies not so much in orthodox psychiatric symptomology and dynamics—which note that some patients suffer from headaches, others from insomnia; that some project, others compensate; that some are paranoid, others schizophrenic. Rather, the difference lies in the life patterns that evoke suffering. Southern Protestant Ethic patients will be bothered by patterns and problems of one type, Classical Protestants by patterns and problems of another type.

Deducing from the Classical Protestant pattern, one might suspect that its adherents will tend to feel guilty about poor planning and poor implementation of plans pertaining to long segments of life— projects and careers. They will see their failurees as composing a methodical and relentlessly cumulative build-up toward collapse. If they worry about drink, sex, gambling and other personal vices, they worry about them specifically as distractions from the straight and narrow path toward achievement and service for God or some secular surrogate of God. Installment plans, savings accounts, career plans, and growth rates are worries to the Classical Protestant Ethic patient.

Deducing from the Southern Protestant pattern, one suspects that its adherents balance hope for instant salvation with fear of instant damnation or secular equivalents thereof. Their guilt or shame derives less from systematic and continuous movement toward collapse than from one or more discrete and traumatic lapses or goofs. A rape of or by oneself, a sexual affair of self or spouse, a drunken episode, a social faux pas, a failure of nerve in a particular confrontation, as in battle, brawl, or football, will torment the Southern Protestant Ethic patient. Such failures occur in relation to specific persons, often hometown neighbors or relatives perceived as either opponents or disapproving spectators. The Classical Protestant patient's failure and guilt are more closely related to an abstract life plan or reference group, such as his profession.

Symptoms of the Classical Protestant patient might tend toward the delusional. He may tend to elaborate goal-oriented schemes, as did one Northern-born patient I interviewed. This fellow literally perceived life as a giant baseball field and was anxious about his inability to reach second base. Obsessive-compulsive scheduling should neatly express the Classical Protestant emphasis on specialized purity. By compulsively meticulous separation of the specialized thrust of work from the diffuse and disorderly miasma of personal relations, the thrust is purified. In Puritan imagery, this thrust is God's tool, so that polishing, purifying, and streamlining it by compulsive scheduling are essential

Symptoms of the Southern patient apparently tend toward conversion hysteria, as in imagined paralysis and pain. The Classical Protestant patient will perhaps tend less toward bodily hysteria. For him, body is merely an instrument of service to God. Bodily adornment is not so much evil as inefficient, and if it should prove efficient it would presumably be allowed. More absolute is the Southerner's attitude toward adornment of body and person. He is either totally for it, as in the Southern Cavalier or Southern beauty queen complexes, or he is totally against it, as in the harsh taboos of fundamentalists. Not surprisingly, the fundamentalists, who taboo makeup, manifest symptoms such as those displayed by one woman I interviewed. Her cheeks ached unbearably where she had worn rouge. Southern patients may generally focus their symptoms more around the adornment and contour of the body than do Classical Protestant patients.

The Classical Protestant patient's anxieties should, according to the logic of the Classical Ethic, flow more from friends, neighbors, and co-workers, whereas the Southerner's anxieties should derive more from blood kin. Social science suggests that the middle-class Classical Protestant son's fears and anxieties will focus around a mother who withholds love except when the son achieves (McClelland 1967:340-362). Research suggests that the Southern patient's fears will derive more from an authoritarian father—the type who administers whippings to a wayward son (Morland 1958:90-92).

The personalistic warp of the Southern Protestant Ethic can be expected to encourage what Tom Wolfe calls a "good ol' boy" ethic (1966). Patients will worry about not being good ol' boys, being mean and ugly instead of nice to people. Classical Protestants are encouraged by their belief to act mean and ugly in the name of reform for the sake of God, or His plan, or some other transcendent purpose; hence they might worry less about being nasty but worry more about not contributing to some abstract godly and social aim. Especially the Classical patient may worry and feel anxious about choosing a socially useless job.

Given the violence of Southern Protestant Ethic patterns of salvation, the Southern patient's disease, conceived as damnation, should tend toward violence. He should display more violent symptoms than the Classical patient, who should tend more toward systematic and compulsive intellectualization and scheduling. A careful analysis of the timing of symptoms might reveal that Classical Protestant patients degenerate more methodically and systematically, whereas Southerners fall apart by violent and erratic outbursts.

A word should be said now about the methods that will be employed to diagnose these two diseases within a population of patients. A questionnaire, partly derived from the foregoing deductions, is being administered to patients entering a certain section of Butner hospital during the next few months. Some of the items on the questionnaire will induce patients to classify themselves as more of the Classical Protestant or of the Southern Protestant religious persuasion. Other items portray life problems that seem logically to derive from one of the other of the two traditions. Possibly patients who classify themselves as Classical Protestant in religious orientation will consistently choose a configuration of life problems that contrasts with the configuration chosen by the Southern Protestant patients. Conceivably these contrasting configurations will resemble the sketch of diseases just presented—but perhaps not.

Turning from method to implication, a theoretical implication of the proposed study can first be noted. If patients embodying the Southern Protestant Ethic do turn out to differ clearly and consistently in mental disease from patients holding to the Classical Protestant Ethic, the utility of Weberian (and Hillian) typologies will be demonstrated in a new sphere—the abnormal. Indeed, it may be that the implications of religious belief in the realm of the irrational, in the spheres of neurosis and psychosis, are stronger than in comparatively rational business, which was Weber's concern.

A second implication of the study is more practical. Some psychiatrists sense that something is different about mental patients who are endowed with the Southern Protestant Ethic. None, so far as I know, have mapped with precision or depth the psychological contours of the Southern Protestant Ethic disease. Failing to understand the sickness, psychiatrists may not fully comprehend the treatment. Psychoanalysis, with its methodical, systematic, and rational progression matches the Classical Protestant pattern of salvation, but not the more episodic, dramatic, and emotional pattern of the Southern Protestant who, according to Hill (1966:85), is accustomed to feel himself "stricken, then released, remorseful then joyful, doomed then pronounced free of condemnation." If patterns of disease match Southern patterns of the Fall, then patterns of treatment should resonate with accustomed Southern patterns of salvation.

## NOTES

1. This paper was originally presented as part of the conference on *The Bible Belt in Continuity and Change,* chaired by Professors Samuel S. Hill and Edgar Thompson, January, 1969, at Chapel Hill and Durham, North Carolina.

## REFERENCES

Hill, Samuel S., Jr., 1966. *Southern Churches in Crisis* (New York: Holt, Rinehart).

McClelland, David C., 1967. *The Achieving Society* (New York: Free Press).

Morland, John Kenneth, 1958. *Millways of Kent* (Chapel Hill: University of North Carolina Press).

Peacock, James L. and A. Thomas Kirsch, 1970. *The Human Direction* (New York: Appleton-Century-Crofts).

Weber, Max, 1958. *The Protestant Ethic and the Spirit of Capitalism* (New York: Scribner's).

Wolfe, Tom, 1966. *Kandy-Kolored, Tangerine Flake, Streamline Baby* (New York: Pocket Books).

# The Southern Way of Death

CHRISTOPHER CROCKER

FUNERALS and weddings are the two great rituals in American life which have most relevance to the individual's understanding of himself in relation to his society.[1] The symbols utilized in each of these rituals serve to define the categories and normative relationships of social life in particularly self-contained, systematic fashion. They also reflect certain beliefs about "final causes," God, the meaning of life, and, generally, the epistomological conditions of human existence. As such they are relevant to any examination of what the South understands itself to be. But one immediate problem is the identification of a uniquely "Southern" way of death. Many of the customs discussed here are preeminently American practices in the most general sense. However any judgment as to the extent of specific identity between Southern funerals and those in other sections of the country is hindered by a lack of precise ethnographic information on the subject. While monographs on the "exploitative" aspects of American funerals have had success (Mitford 1963; Harner 1963), and while there are superb sociological studies of "passing on" in the hospital considered as an American institution (Sudnow 1967), there have been no extended analyses of the social matrix of ceremonies involved with death and the collective representation of death in a modern American community.[2]

This paper is a preliminary effort at filling the gap. It is a report on research in progress, which I hope will stimulate further investigation. I shall not be concerned with the controversy over the high cost, the aesthetic taste, or general social validity of modern funerals, except as the general lack of public concern with such topics in the South is an important aspect of the regional deathways. The absence, for example, of memorial societies in the area as a whole reflects the almost total dominion of the churches over funerals. Rather, the paper's emphasis is on the ways in which death is socially handled

114

as reflected in funeral practices in two Southern communities. My particular concern shall be the nature and relationships between social and moral categories as these emerge in the organized, prescribed procedures of deathways. The last section of the paper will attempt to relate some ideologically problematic aspects of death as presented in Southern funerals to a fundamentalistic and presumably Southern Christian belief system. In short, I shall proceed on the classical anthropological dictum that death is a social process as well as a biological event (Hertz, 1960).

The data presented here have come from interviews among middle and upper-lower class whites and from participant observation in two communities in North Carolina, one a relatively small, homogeneous, and tradition oriented town and the other an expanding, industrialized urban center. While there are differences in practices between the two localities and between sub-groups in each of them, such contrasts are surprisingly minor even though they have considerable significance to actors as definitions of critical group boundaries This is true, for example, for variations between the practices of historical churches and the chiliastic sects. However, critical differences, in terms of the actors' perspectives, are found between black and white funeral customs. Indeed, white informants corroborated accounts in the existing literature that a "proper funeral" is defined partly in opposition to the supposed characteristics of black funerals. While a comparison of the two types would be illuminating, black deathways have been excluded from consideration here through lack of space and data.

With this exception, the near identity of the practices of all classes and sects, even Catholics and Jews, has considerable analytical importance. Since there are shared expectations as to the appropriate sequence of events and the "proper" behavior during the funeral, persons from distinct segments of the community may participate in the ritual. But the common definition of a "proper funeral" —that is, one which follows a single prescribed normative pattern— derives from a number of factors and certainly cannot be accounted for on the basis of any supposed functional consequence of fostering community solidarity. Furthermore, the similarity of the deathways in the communities studied should not be taken to imply any such identity throughout the South. Even though references will be made to "Southern" rather than "Carolinian," generalizations from the towns studied to the region as a whole should be made with some caution.

I

The following account shall deal first with the customs surrounding the process of dying and death itself; next, with the
separate phases of the funeral as defined by the actors; and last,
with the nature of mourning, the status and contemporary relevance
of the dead in the community, and the symbolic values reflected in
the cemetery. It must first be noted that today nearly all Southerners
either die in a hospital or during the process of dying are passed
through the organization of the modern hospital. Indeed, "going to
the hospital" has apparently come to signify dying for many middle
and lower class Southerners. This has considerable significance since
the hospital involves a set of structural and ideological elements which
serve to interpret and to define the exact nature of dying for society.
Sudnow's recent work in a hospital in a large West Coast city is
quite relevant here, for the hospital's characteristics do not appear to
vary a great deal from region to region. He points out that dying
is not a medically appropriate disease category or even symptom in
the way that cancer or fibrillation is. The hospital's application of
the category of "dying" to a given patient must be carefully judged by
the doctors and administrators. If used early in the case it may imply to
relatives and others that medical efforts have been curtailed too soon,
particularly if the patient continues to live for some time. But it
is also crucial that the term be applied in advance of actual death,
because it conveys the meaning that all that could be done has been
done, and that a natural process is underway that no human agency
can control. Therefore the doctor must convey the impression that
death is always possible although everything is being done to prevent
it (Sudnow 1967:90-99). The doctor's problem of maintaining a
credible ambiguity, endemic in his role, seems less acute in the communities studied than elsewhere, perhaps because of the common
local belief that illness, recovery, or death are all reflections of God's
plan. While the sufficient cause of death is admitted to be an auto
accident or cancer or cessation of heart beat, the necessary cause
is always divine will.[3] Furthermore, my observations indicate that the
common American ambivalence toward doctors is less strong in the
South, at least in terms of overt attitudes among lower and lower
middle class whites. This in turn may be related to the same belief,
in that doctors are regarded as themselves agents of the Holy Will,
or to regional notions of the respect due any professional, or com-
binations of these with other factors.

The actual application of the "dying" category to a patient initiates the rite of passage that is the Southern funeral: it sets in motion

a chain of patterned sequential actions and attitudes beginning with preparation for the announcement that death has occurred. Thus, "dying" is regarded as a private rather than a public matter, and therefore only those considered nearest the afflicted person are informed of the gravity of the situation. Most classes in the two communities, however, also felt it very important that the "immediate relatives" (the definition of this category is considered below) be present at the end. Indeed, in the South the horror of dying alone is matched only by that of being buried alone or in an unmarked grave. The former attitude appears based on the assumption that the dying man can be reassured by the presence of his "loved ones." In part, at least, the practice is a Southern one; in larger metropolitan hospitals it has been noted that visiting tapers off sharply after the "dying" category is applied (Sudnow 1967:72-77), whereas in North Carolina the reverse appears to be the case. This, however, is one of the last times in the funeral sequence that explicit attention is given to maintaining or fostering certain states in the dying or dead person. As anthropologists have known since Mauss, funeral practices in many other societies are explicitly devoted to securing various conditions for the deceased's soul in the transition from this world to the afterlife. But in the South, after this first act, the totality of ritual concern is with the living. Even here, certain categories of relatives— among them, young children and the elderly—are exempt from the obligation to be present during "dying." The doctor's problematic tightrope is again encountered by the relatives in their preparations during the "dying" to "dead" period, for it is thought vital that such "readying" actions should not proceed too rapidly or extensively —"After all, what would it be like if he got better and the undertaker was already there?" Hence preparation is likely to be very covert and slow, and the family typically resolves the problem by delaying to contact a minister and mortician until the doctor announces, "It is only a matter of time now."[4]

The insistence on the combined services of an undertaker and a preacher is at once an aspect of and a major element in the maintenance of the expected sequence of events and meanings in the funeral. It is considered essential by all informants that the deceased have a "church funeral," regardless of past religious affiliation, moral history, or circumstances of death. With rare exceptions an alcoholic, a suicide, and a child all have *formally* similar funerals. The minister is usually one associated with the deceased's or a relative's particular church; this selection causes problems when family members belong to different churches. There seems to be less difficulty with the chiliastic sects, perhaps due to a tendency for "family" to be defined by co-membership in the church. The mortician is usually chosen by a combination of criteria, including co-membership with the family in church, lodge, or other associational group and/or evaluation of his past skill at conducting "proper" funerals. Both prior arrangements contracted by the deceased and the process of "shopping around" for the cheapest funeral on the part of the family are evidently rare in the South, and both appear to be viewed as reprehensible. Perhaps this is true because these activities subvert the notion of the "proper funeral." But regardless of the ways in which preparation has been made, as soon as death occurs the community must be notified. The patterned ways in which the news is conveyed to relatives, friends, associates, and others reflect the normative relationships between these persons and the deceased. These ways establish the differing obligations of roles during the funeral and mourning period. The customary Southern ways of spreading news of a death are very much like those described for other parts of the country (Sudnow 1967:154-168), with some exceptions to be given later.

The first persons notified by those in attendance at the death bed or by the doctor are relatives described as "having the right to know" of the death: spouse, lineal relatives (such as parents, children, and grandparents/grandchildren), and immediate consanguineals such as siblings. There is an emphasis on personal notification, by telephone rather than by public media or by card; thus airlines do not release lists of crash victims until the "relatives," those defined as having the right to know, are informed personally. Those persons having this right and those with the right to grieve and to receive public sympathy are virtually identical; together they compose the rather sharply bounded category designated as "the mourners" or "the immediate family." As Sudnow shows (1967:161-162), this group may also be characterized as those who are entitled to an unqualified use of "my" in describing their relationship to the deceased. Thus someone has only to say, "My father died" to be regarded as a mourner, but a more distant relation must qualify the kinship tie, as with the statement, "My dear sister's boy who was like a son to me," in order to establish his character as one who has suffered direct loss.

The relationship of first order collaterals—uncles, aunts, cousins, nephews, and nieces—to this category seems quite ambiguous. Their "right to know," to be categorized as "immediate family," seems to vary according to the particular kinship system operative in the local society. I have neither the space nor the data to explore this problem in detail. However, it is my impression that in those regions where economic matters (including inheritance and labor exchange) along with political and religious activities are identified as being the responsibility of an extended kindred, such collaterals are included in the "immediate family." Concomitantly, as the socially significant kin group is more or less restricted to lineal relatives with an emphasis on the nuclear family, the collaterals are of course excluded. In a very general way, the two modes of grouping might be characterized as rural (and Southern) and urban (and Northern) if it is realized that both modes can be found in the same community or region.

The death practices discussed above constitute one important way in which a person's membership in different kin groups is defined. For example, those relatives who fail to comply with the normative requirements of their kinship relationships lose the right to be relatives, to be regarded as family members. Thus a cruel, profligate, or "sinful" son may not be informed immediately of his parent's death. The manner and time in which persons outside the immediate family are notified of the death is also highly significant. It has been pointed out that, "It is possible to learn a good deal about a person's position in a variety of social structures by mapping out the circles of those persons entitled to learn about his death" (Sudnow 1967: 154). Thus it is considered improper that individuals learn of the death from others more distantly related to the deceased, so that a first cousin should not be told by an in-law. Therefore the family attempts to have each circle of relations inform each other: friends tell friends, cousins tell cousins and so forth. Complex factors of status in the local community, moral judgments, rights and obligations implicit in different roles, all influence the sequence of events.

The process of notification is complicated by the fact, as Sudnow demonstrates, that those who are regarded as immediately bereaved and entitled to sympathy are hindered from informing persons in the non-bereaved categories, for to do so would create a complex problem in interaction. To inform a friend that one's father has died requires the friend to extend sympathy and may be interpreted as a claim to such sympathy. Further, behavior toward the bereaved and acts expressing regard for the deceased should ideally be similar to gifts, things which must have a free, spontaneous quality however much they are normatively enjoined. So while members of "the immediate family" may inform each other, they cannot tell anyone else; the responsibility for imparting the news to the next circle of kin is usually taken by an affinal relative, such as the husband of the deceased's sister. Often there is an explicit division of labor, with the caller instructing the respondent to tell certain others. In this way judgments as to the deceased's position in a variety of social units as well as the nature of his relationships with persons in those units continue to be made throughout the process of notification.

Two final points need to be made here: first, the act of mourning is always associated with "blood ties," with close biological relationships as these are perceived by the local society. The community's loss of a member is portrayed dominantly as a biological matter, not as one of presumed social value. This is related to the insistence that all persons have the right to a "proper" church funeral. Since this ritual is thought more for the mourners' than the deceased's benefit, it is the only appropriate structure for the expression of grief. Second, the obligation to inform certain persons immediately reflects a concern that their social demeanor be congruent with the "fact" of death. This concern, as expressed in such statements as, "She was dancing and singing as her mother lay dead," is related to the problems of ambiguity found in Southern symbolic representations of the dead that shall be discussed at the conclusion of the paper.

## II

The funeral itself is separated into four quite distinct phases, each with its particular social configurations and symbolism. These phases are the wake, which removes the deceased along with the bereaved from society and secular existence; second, the "visiting" in the funeral parlor, a period of ambiguous non-social time which continues nearly unbroken into the third phase, the church service. Finally the fourth stage, burial at the cemetery, incorporates the deceased into the company of the dead and signals the beginning of the mourners' assumption of their normal secular roles. These analytical processes of separation from the society, a marginal period of transition, and finally re-incorporation are derived from van Gennep's historic formulation of the sequence in rites of passage (1960).

The wake is an old custom which seems to be common in the traditional community studied but which is disappearing in the urban center. In holding a wake the "immediate family" does not go to bed on the night following the death, but is at home to callers. The underlying assumption is that the bereaved are too upset to sleep and require extensive social support since they are incapacitated by grief and unable to fulfill normal roles. Therefore the visitors bring great amounts of food. Those kin, neighbors, and friends who are considered to be outside the bereaved category assume domestic chores as well as those funeral arrangements not part of the mortician's duties. The mourners, as defined in the ways indicated above, are expected to demonstrate fairly standardized signs of grief. Women should cry and "take on" generally; even mild hysterics are not socially disapproved. Men should exhibit an outward composure while indicating through various recognized and stereotyped signs their actual emotional states. Under no circumstances should mourners attempt to "carry on as usual," nor is the Southern wake ever characterized by the joking and revelry which supposedly occur during similar rituals in other American regions. The stress on the inappropriateness of usual roles is one more reflection of the separation of the mourners from society.

The food brought by the callers at the wake is limited not in quantity but in variety. It appears that in the South, rites of passage are marked by the consumption of special ceremonial foods. These consist, at least for the areas studied, of smoked or country ham, sliced white chicken or turkey meat, potato salad, and cakes and pies of various types. Other items certainly do appear, and there are no explicit prohibitions or prescriptions such as found in the ceremonial diets of other societies. Rather, there is a vague feeling that the above dishes are somehow appropriate to ritual occasions. The reasons for this association are quite complex and deserve further research. One possible mode of analysis would be to focus on the total field of man-animal relationships in the South, endeavoring to discover if pigs and chickens are considered to have any sort of special relationship to their owners.[5]

Interestingly, the social categories expected to attend the wake are not clearly defined, in the sense that there are no normative expectations as to who should or should not come. Attendance, then, becomes another way in which membership in social units can be expressed and the deceased's social position revealed freely, without the constraint of prescribed behavior. In practice, the persons attending the wake are those who categorize themselves, and expect to be classified, as intensely affected by the death due to closeness of relationship to the deceased or to those directly bereaved. The wake is explicitly private, a family matter, and thus contrasts with the public ceremonies which follow it. Thus it is characterized by an emphasis on particularistic and functionally diffuse relationships. It is significant that business associates, friends, lodge members, fellow churchmen and those in other functionally specific roles make an appearance during the Southern wake, for in so doing they stress the diffuse and unique quality of their relations with the deceased and his family. In contrast, those persons who call on the family during the period between the wake and the burial, when the bereaved are similarly at home to the community, are proclaiming a somewhat more distant relationship. These latter visitors, then, may be regarded as members of the broad category of "sympathizers," those who attend the funeral parlor and/or the church service.

III

During the next two phases the family occupies a marginal status which must be demonstrated by aspects of their conduct, such as clothing. Currently in the South, any public viewing of the body or casket, if done at all, occurs at a funeral home rather than in the deceased's own house, as was formerly the case. This event comes from one to three or four days after death, and lasts for only a morning or afternoon. Its public quality is reflected in the announcements of the event through the mass media. Persons of the "immediate family" should be present to receive condolences, although very often the individuals regarded as most afflicted, such as a wife or mother, are exempt from this obligation. The two elements of the ritual viewing which seem most significant to me are the presentations of flowers and the importance attached to a last view of the body, which is made to look as nondead as possible.

It is somewhat surprising that all informants said there was no particular symbolic importance in the variety of flowers used. Rather, it is form, size, and quantity of the "floral tributes" which are emphasized. The different types of such gifts are loosely associated with particular social categories. "Standing wreaths" are given by members of the immediate family, according to the ways in which this group has been defined during the preceding phrase. Therefore the contribution of such displays by others, whether families, individuals, or groups, becomes a social declaration of the closeness of relationship to the deceased and, consequently, of the importance of the loss suffered. That is, to give a standing wreath is to say, "The deceased was like a member of our family." When an important community figure dies he or she may receive wreaths from a variety of organizations, but it may be stretching a point to say that the deceased is thus declared a town father or mother. Sprays, again a unique arrangement used only at funerals, are contributed by relatives, friends, neighbors, colleagues, and the like, those who have suffered loss but who are not regarded as "bereaved." The bier is contributed only by the "immediate family."

The symbolism involved with the "floral tributes" is at least two-fold. First, the specific forms of the wreaths are often explicit statements—a "bleeding heart" or "unbroken circle." Second, the presentation of flowers in American society is generally associated with the affirmation of affectual solidarity, of feeling so intense that it may be expressed in no other type of gift but flowers. Women are usually taken to be vehicles and objects of such feeling, so that the institution of "flower girls" is an important element in Southern working class funerals. These women convey the floral tributes from cars into the church, and from the church to the graveside. They are usually drawn from an important referent group of the deceased, such as an adult Sunday School class, or a school class in the case of a dead child or adolescent, or some club, such as Eastern Star. For male deceased, the group is often chosen on the basis of the wife's associational membership. In all cases, only women actually handle the flowers. On a more sociological level, the flower girls are expected to remove the tags indicating the donor or donors, and note the type of floral offering and its form on the reverse side. These tags are given to the immediate family so that a formal note of appreciation can later be sent to the givers. The analogy to wedding presents is striking.[6] While the general public does not usually see the tags (although in some areas these are left attached), there is a general correlation drawn between the number, size, and approximate cost of the flowers and the deceased's social position. This sort of evaluation of the funeral occurs throughout the ritual, and there appears to be considerable preoccupation on the part of the bereaved with such judgments of size and cost. One of the critical elements of a "proper funeral" is that it be deemed in these terms congruent with the deceased's and his family's social position.

The concern with the lifelike appearance of the corpse, and the stress on the "last view" which accompanies it, is often claimed to be a bit of astute salesmanship by undertakers. I doubt this is the case. Rather, the morticians have responded to a widely held value, particularly in the South. This is not so much an attempt to deny the reality of death as to present it as a phase of life. It may not be too much of an imaginative leap to say that the collective representation of death as a type of peaceful sleep is an assertion that the dead have a special kind of life. This can only be assured them through the cosmetic manipulations of embalming, the purchase of which is a moral obligation of their descendants. Certain aspects of the American cemetery, such as its characterization as a garden and a place of waiting, support, I think, this interpretation.

The visiting period at the funeral parlor shades into the church service, and, in fact, the two rites are often combined. Here the symbols used in hymns and prayers focus on the moral character of death in general, as well as its particular significance in terms of the deceased's life. I will deal with this at the end of the paper, along with the problem of the selection of appropriate eulogies, hymns, and so forth for morally ambiguous categories such as suicides, infants, and alcoholics. But first, the social categories involved in the church service and burial must be examined. In addition to the flower girls, another critical social unit appears at the service itself, the pallbearers. Members of this group are usually selected from among the deceased's close friends, business associates, and nonbereaved kin, or in the case of a dead woman, from her husband's associates and relatives. Again the exact composition of this group reflects the totality of social roles held by the deceased, and of course it forms the masculine counterpart of the flower girls. Older men or those who are regarded as physically incapacitated from carrying the coffin are designated as honorary pallbearers, and in fact this may present a delicate problem since men may object to such a categorization. Generally, the pattern of southern funerals appears to stress the incorporation into the ritual of a great many otherwise discrete, functionally specialized, and well differentiated social groups. The boundaries between these units are eclipsed by the sense of common loss, so that the funeral becomes a time when mechanical rather than organic solidarity is emphasized.

This stress is further reflected in the very strongly enjoined obligation for the deceased's relatives, friends, colleagues, associates, and neighbors—in short all those who are regarded as having participated significantly in the deceased's life—to attend the funeral in a proper ritual condition. By this last term I mean that the appropriate inner emotional state should be reflected in dress and deportment, in the wearing of best clothes, a diffuse attitude of grave seriousness, and so forth. As one informant put it, "Everyone has to have a clean white shirt to go to funerals in." The obligation to attend the funeral is decreasingly binding the further the formal social distance from the deceased, but it obtains for "immediate family" regardless of the actual facts of the relationship. Two brothers may not have spoken for twenty years, but one is obligated to go to the other's funeral. One of the most damning moral classifications a Southerner can apply is, "He's so mean he didn't (or wouldn't) go to his own mother's funeral." Not to comply with this requirement is to place oneself beyond society in a quite definitive way. It is significant that one of the critical episodes in the career of a folk hero-criminal (as presented in a song or movie) is his presence, incognito, at a relative's funeral.

## IV

The burial itself is generally regarded as the most traumatic phase of the entire ritual, and during it various kinds of emotional outbursts are expected and usually condoned. This may be due to the character of the burial as the particular rite which begins the process of incorporation of the bereaved into normal society, and which moves the deceased into the company of the dead. The persons who attend the burial are usually those who participated in the wake, so that we find a blurring of the public-private distinction in the concluding as at the initial portion of this rite of passage. The actual location of the plot involves a statement of the deceased's critical social affiliations. Thus a wife is buried by her husband, but a daughter by her parents. It seems clear that American cemeteries emphasize lineal kinship ties. The only exception to this rule occurs not so much as a consequence of moral judgments—for the black sheep of the family ultimately will lie in the family plot—but as when the circumstances of death are thought to involve even higher values than those represented by the family. Soldiers are buried together, patriotism being the highest good of all,[7] and sometimes other associational groups predominate over particularistic values, as when the three or four adolescent victims of an automobile crash are placed in the same separate plot. Above all, however, the deceased's burial site must have some social referent, so that he is assigned at the end, as throughout the funeral, some universal and perpetual category. A pauper's grave, an unmarked site, is hideous because it is a complete end to all the social categories embodied by the dead man. This, as we have known since Durkheim, is a fundamental threat to the very basis of social cohesion.

There are no definite sets of mourning rules, which is surprising until we consider the flexibility such imprecision allows for the demonstration of "actually felt," as opposed to socially enjoined, feelings and attitudes. Up to this point the actions and even the precise social composition of the bereaved group has been restricted by normative expectations. The freedom to mourn allows two things: the socially defined bereaved have the opportunity to demonstrate that they do indeed feel grief and do not merely act a role. Second, those more distantly related to the deceased may show that in emotional fact the relationship was closer than its formal characteristics indicated, that a business associate was indeed "like a son to me." At the other extreme, and typically Southern, is a normative stress on the consistency of demonstrated grief during the ceremony and of conduct during the following period. For example, a widow who "cuts **up** awful" during the burial service and then remarries some six months later is subject to considerable adverse sanctions. This appears to be another implicit recognition of the possibility of hypocritical compliance with role expectations. This threatens solidarity, which rests on the paradox that to be an effective base of social cohesion, shared emotional states must be at once free and obligatory.

Perhaps the most striking ideological characteristic of Southern funerals, as represented in the material presented here, is their explicit avoidance of moral or theological judgments. Funerals are for the living, not the dead, and the ways in which these rituals are conducted have only social rather than cosmological significance. As I mentioned earlier, a suicide and even a murderer have the right to "a proper funeral" just like that of an individual revered throughout the community for his saintly conduct. To be sure, the community response may well demonstrate their judgment of the moral worth of such persons, but the point is, first, that each of them receive formally the same kind of treatment, and second, that neither the moral character of the deceased nor the specific incidents of a particular funeral affects the condition of the soul in the afterlife. Each of these elements, from anthropology's perspective, is unusual and intriguing, and in my view they relate first to certain features of Southern religion and next to various aspects of death as a social phenomenon. Charles Hudson has demonstrated that in fundamentalistic Southern Christian belief, illness and dying are held to be the primary instrumentality of supernatural justice.[8] The death of a wild, sinful boy in a car accident and the almost miraculous recovery of an elderly Christian woman are held to be examples of God's judgments and the direct consequence of sin and salvation. At the same time, the proper Christian who is visited by boils, economic calamities, and finally an early death is considered an example of fate, an act of God which cannot, and should not, be comprehended by man. Illness, suffering, and death are represented in the South as human tribulations during which faith may be demonstrated: they are "trials," in a very literal sense.

The important point is that no matter how much sinners as an abstract category may be consigned to everlasting hellfire, in the funeral no *particular* sinner is portrayed as suffering such pangs of the damned. Not only practice, but books of instruction for funerals written by Southern ministers for their regional colleagues insist that the most morally reprehensible of persons should be pictured during the burial service as enjoying the fruits of salvation. This is deemed a proper and fitting response not so much for the immediate family's sake, but in terms of doctrine and faith. The emphasis of hymns and eulogies is on the mysterious ways of God's will, and the necessity of avoiding moral judgments concerning the ontological status of the deceased. In the cemetery the dead are portrayed as morally equal and of similar relevance for the living: they are "all family." This may strike an anthropologist from another culture as an excellent demonstration of the logical inconsistencies in what Levy-Bruhl termed mystical participations, but I do not think this is the case. In Southern society, moral classifications stop at the grave, and this is one particular way of handling a perhaps universal human problem: the ambiguity of death.

From an individual standpoint, social time is serial, non-repetitive, yet from the position of society this must not be the case (Evans-Pritchard 1940:94-95). To admit that what has happened may not happen again, that the passing of an individual creates a vacuum which may never be filled up, is to admit the falseness of social categories and the vulnerability of social processes. This threatens the entire expectational system, which is based on the assumption of cyclic rhythms. Thus funerals must resolve an inherent ambiguity: the sense of uniqueness of an individual's life and the enduring quality of the roles he filled and which may now be filled by others. The emphasis during the funeral on the living and even on their obligation to the deceased to continue the process of social existence is one aspect of the resolution of this ambiguity. In more specific ways, the reiteration of the dead man's character in terms of his specific biological roles, that of father, son, husband, nephew, and grandfather, affirms the universality and inevitability of these positions. At the most, as when a young child dies, the manner and time of death conjoined with the moral *persona* of the deceased may be represented as a trial for the living, a period during which their faith may be tested. But the explicit refusal to judge the dead also carries with it the assertion that life has no definite end either in the glories of heaven or the pangs of hell, but instead continues, indefinitely and ambiguously. Thus we find in the funeral the affirmation of all the statueses and roles through which the deceased played out his social game, along with the assertion that social existence is indeed perpetual, enduring, and cyclic. The Southern way of death is therefore one way of preserving the continuity of Southern life.[9]

## NOTES

1. A prior version of this paper was read at a conference entitled "The Bible Belt in Continuity and Change," sponsored by the Center for Southern

Studies of Duke University and held in January, 1969. I wish to express my gratitude to James Peacock, Charles Hudson, and Edgar Thompson for both their general comments on Southern religion and for their suggestions regarding this paper. I am particularly indebted to Mr. Leonard Kovit and to my wife, Eleanor Crocker, for their numerous suggestions and insights concerning Southern funerals. The views expressed here are of course my own responsibility.

2. While various community studies include some notes on the local character of funerals, the topic is not systematically investigated or analyzed. Perhaps the most extended and systematic analysis is to be found in Warner's *The Family of God* (1961:157-260). However, Warner's material is somewhat dated and the treatment neglects the social categories and groupings discussed here.

3. As might be suspected, this faith sometimes encounters difficulties in encompassing suicides, murders, and "freak" accidents. I have heard these tragedies attributed to the Devil's machinations, even though it is generally recognized that this is not accepted by religious authorities. Since the paper was written, a murder has occurred in the traditional community, and public opinion seems to be that the accused (the victim's husband) should *not* have a "proper funeral" whenever and however he dies.

4. It is perhaps obvious that sudden death, particularly when it occurs to the young, is all the more difficult to accept because it has no similar "preparation time." The apparent tendency for the funerals in these cases to be more protracted and elaborate may be an attempt to provide *post facto* a period of adjustment.

5. These comments derive, of course, from recent theories concerning liminal, anomalous animal categories put forward by various anthropologists (Leach 1964; Douglas 1966).

6. There are other analogies between funerals and weddings; perhaps the most striking is the Southern custom of burying women in "peignoirs" especially made for this purpose. This might be interpreted as congruent with the "death as sleep" view discussed below, but several informants made explicit comparisons between this garment and similar ones in a bride's trousseau.

7. Recently some men killed in Vietnam have been buried with their families, with the explicit reason that the war there is "bad" and "wrong."

8. Charles Hudson, "The Structure of a Fundamentalist Belief System," in Samuel Hill (ed.), *Religion and the Solid South*, forthcoming.

9. Comments on earlier drafts of this paper stressed that many of the practices discussed are not unique to the South, and that customs of different social classes are considerably more heterogeneous than I assume. Both assertions may reflect the current situation in Southern urban centers, in which there has been rapid social change for the past two decades.

## REFERENCES

Douglas, Mary, 1966. *Purity and Danger* (London: Routledge and Kegan Paul).

Evans-Pritchard, E. E., 1940. *The Nuer* (Oxford: Clarendon Press).

Harner, R., 1963. *The High Cost of Dying* (New York: Crowell, Collier, and Macmillan).

Hertz, Robert, 1960. *Death and the Right Hand* (Glencoe, Ill.: The Free Press).

Leach, Edmund, 1964. Anthropological Aspects of Language: Animal Categories and Verbal Abuse. In *New Directions in the Study of Language*, E. H. Lenneberg, ed. (Cambridge: M. I. T. Press), pp. 23-63.

Mitford, Jessica, 1963. *The American Way of Death* (New York: Simon and Schuster).

Sudnow, David, 1967. *Passing On* (Englewood Cliffs, N. J.: Prentice-Hall).

van Gennep, A., 1960. *The Rites of Passage* (Chicago: Phoenix Books).

Warner, W. Lloyd, 1961. *The Family of God* (New Haven: Yale University Press).

# Conclusion: Problems and Prospects

J. Kenneth Morland

The call for more anthropological study of American culture and society has sometimes been put on the basis that it is a necessary move because of the eventual disappearance of the preliterate societies and cultures which have primarily been the province of anthropologists. Thus, both John Gillin (1967) and Leslie White (1965) sounded this note in recent presidential addresses to the American Anthropological Association. Gillin stated that whether they liked it or not cultural anthropologists were being drawn into the study of complex industrial societies. White raised the question of what the ethnographer would do when preliterate societies were gone. He felt that diminishing returns were setting in from continual studies of some tribes and that the remark that a Zuni household consisted of mother, father, children, and a social anthropologist was not entirely a joke. Furthermore, he thought that trivialities were being dealt with in some anthropological journal articles, such as "An Unusual Prayer-stick from Acoma Pueblo," and "The Excavation of Hopewell Site Number 793." While disclaiming the intention of saying that anthropologists should not be interested in such details, he wondered if more valuable and significant studies could be made. Both he and Gillin urged cultural anthropologists to study American society, thus enlarging their scope to cover the entire field of culture which is rightfully theirs.

An even more valid justification than moving into its "rightful field" is the special contribution anthropology can make to the understanding of modern, complex societies. These societies have long been the domain of sociology, political science, and economics, and these disciplines have developed concepts and research techniques designed to deal with the complexities of urban societies. We need to make sure that anthropology is not merely duplicating the efforts of sociologists and others, but, rather, that it is making a unique contribution. Max Gluckman and Fred Eggan have reminded us of what this contribution can be by pointing out that in addition to their traditional emphasis on tribal societies anthropologists have in common:

> . . . a continuing focusing of interest on customs, as having an interrelated dependence on one another, whether in forming cultural patterns, or in operating within systems of social relations, or in the structuring of various types of personality in different groups. This focus on customs in interdependence has continued to distinguish the disciplines of anthropology from the other subjects with which each branch is increasingly associated (1966:xii).

What Gluckman and Eggan are saying, as I understand it, is that the distinguishing characteristic of anthropological study is the viewing of behavior in its cultural setting. In other words, it is the "holistic" approach. Closely related is the notion of *in vivo* study, as Conrad Arensberg has termed it, that is, study through direct observation and comparison, in contrast to *in vitro* study through isolation and statistical abstraction (1954:110). There are formidable problems in utilizing holistic, *in vivo* research in American society and culture.[1] In the pages which follow we shall look at some of these problems in relation to the papers in this volume, and we shall then consider next steps for anthropological research in the American South.

## Problems of Anthropological Study of American Culture

The first problem in doing research on American culture is selecting the group or type of behavior to be studied. This is not easily or readily done when one intends to employ anthropological approaches in an industrial, urban society. The reports in this volume offer examples of small, distinct groups that might be studied by lone investigators with a minimum of funds. In addition, there are other occupational enclaves like the urban mill people studied by Duncan and the coal miners studied by Knipe and Lewis, other religious sects like the one observed by Keber, other peasant settlements like those delineated by Newton, and additional "gypsy" or itinerant groups as Harper himself suggested. In the last section of this paper a proposal for more systematic and cooperative research will be given.

Acceptance by those being studied is the next problem in anthropological research. Participant-observation requires that the field worker enter into the lives of those he is studying much more than is the case in *in vitro* study. Of course, this is a problem that faces the anthropological field worker regardless of where his study is being conducted.[2] Whether or not it is a greater problem for the anthropologist studying American society than it is for the anthropologist studying tribal society would itself be a valuable topic for research. Americans have become especially sensitive to being studied, regarding it as an invasion of privacy, and this sensitivity is becoming especially acute among minority and other disadvantaged groups in the United States. Obviously, gaining acceptance is by no means easy for Americans studying their own culture. In this volume Gordon and Hodges had surprisingly little difficulty in gaining acceptance by those involved in illegal activity, while, on the other hand, Harper makes a strong point of the necessity of help from a priest who worked with the Irish Travelers, and Keber tells of the breakthrough when she was vouched for by someone trusted by the healing cult. Stanton reports that his position as a community worker led to his acceptance by the Houma. In my own study of the mill village sections of a Southern town, I encountered a great deal of suspicion at the beginning (1958:3). Towards the end of the twelve months of field work, I learned that there had been rumors at various times that I was a company spy, a labor organizer, a private detective, an F. B. I. agent, and a communist. I also learned that if someone were seen talking to me, he was later taunted by fellow mill villagers with, "I see you've been feeding the spy." Gaining genuine acceptance and trust are things that every anthropological field-worker has to strive for throughout his research, whether it is conducted in his own or in another culture.

Another problem of anthropological study of one's own society is that of familiarity with what is being studied. Many anthropologists have felt that in participant-observation it is not possible for the researcher to have the proper perspective and objectivity when studying a culture of which he is a part. They believe there is a real danger of overlooking significant behavior because of being so close to it. As Margaret Mead has put it, students of anthropology have been sent to live in remote societies "to be exposed to ways of behavior quite different from our own, so different in fact that no effort of mind will work that simply redefines the new ways in terms of the known old ways" (1949:25). However, the reports in this volume give every appearance of objectivity, insight, and perspective. Of course, it might be argued that the ways of healing cult members, gypsies, moonshiners, hippies, renegades, miners, pottery-makers, peasants, and mill workers were unfamiliar to the investigators; yet it must be added that members of these groups share much of their culture. And it might be added further that herein lies a major asset, for one important aspect of the culture shared is language. One might wonder just how much would have been missed by Partridge as he listened to conversations in the hippie ghetto, or by Sayers as he interviewed potters, or by Keber as she participated in healing ceremonies, if they had not known the language and had had to work through interpreters.[3] It might be noted, parenthetically, that in participant-observation studies in remote societies anthropologists frequently rely upon informants and translators who are themselves highly familiar with both the culture and the language. In other words, they must see the culture, in part at least, through the eyes of those who are highly familiar with it. At the same time, anthropologists distinguish between behavior that is observed and verbalizations about behavior. Yet, if one believes that language is a "vehicle of the culture" (Herskovits 1955: 277-301), then the field worker who knows the language, including its shades of meanings, innuendoes, and subtleties, has a distinct advantage in describing and analyzing the culture. Of course, anthropologists studying the kinds of groups reported on in this volume undoubtedly encounter some difficulties in understanding the shades of meaning of the English being used, a problem particularly acute in Keber's study of a Black healing sect; but these investigators no doubt understand far more of the language in these studies of the American South than investigators in foreign societies.

As cited above, Gluckman and Eggan emphasize that a special contribution of anthropology is to show the interrelatedness of customs. If one thinks of interrelatedness in terms of American culture as a whole, or even of the Southern regional subculture as a whole, the task is beyond anthropological *in vivo* study at present. America and the American South are simply too complex, too heterogeneous, too little studied for aspects of behavior to be seen fully in context. Perhaps this is what Margaret Lantis had in mind when she said that some anthropologists think that "when we study complex contemporary civilization, we tend to abandon the tenets of our discipline" (1955:1118). Some anthropologists believe that anthropologists who study American society and culture become, in effect, sociologists, since *in vivo*, holistic studies of such a complex culture are virtually impossible. I do not agree, and I feel that research in this volume gives leads as to how the holistic problem may be approached.

One way is to restrict severely the group or type of behavior being considered, as was done in most of the studies in this volume. Thus the context will be so limited that it is possible to see interrelationships within it. Admittedly, this modifies the usual meaning of "holistic," especially since it is unlikely that the groups that are so distinct are typical of the South. But if enough of these groups and behavior patterns are studied comparatively, knowledge about similarity and difference in relationship can be broadened. A more effective approach to being holistic is to use the community as the context, something that will be considered in the last part of this chapter.

Anthropologists who carry out the kinds of studies found in this volume are sometimes accused of being impressionistic, of generalizing from too few or too imprecise data. The problem of generalizing is a constant one for the cultural anthropologist, as indeed it is for every scientific discipline, although perhaps more for the participant-observer than for those who make extensive use of random sampling and official statistical data. Anthropologists have rightly feared over-simplification in trying to generalize from their limited studies to American society as a whole. However, the accusation of being impressionistic is not justified in the case of careful *in vivo* studies. The papers in this volume are based on extensive, careful observation and not on casual impressions, although some contain more systematic, extensive data-gathering than others—for example, the Knipe-Lewis study of coal miners.

A basic purpose of anthropological research is to delineate the culture patterns in the group. Margaret Mead (1953) has pointed out that sampling for the purpose of establishing patterns is different from sampling to determine the extent of variation within patterns, the kind of sampling with which sociologists are especially concerned. According to Mead, the anthropologist assumes that he is dealing with a system that can be delineated by the analysis of a small number of highly specified cases. As an example, she states that this is what the linguist does in determining the structure of a language. There is some risk in this assumption, as Mandelbaum (1953) points out in his argument that language has far less leeway for variation than other aspects of culture. He goes on to say that the only way to be sure that the pattern is really a pattern is to test to see if it recurs under a range of various kinds of observations.

Admittedly, the generalizations offered in the brief reports in this volume are tentative, and the authors call for further research to test them. It is clear that they recognize the difficulty of generalizing from their observations. Even so, problems arise in their reports, as for example in Duncan's study of urban mill workers. After concentrating his attention on the behavior of one family in the mill village area, he raises the question of whether or not the behavior in that family is "typical" of other mill workers. He then declares such a question to be "incongruous," stating that the behavior of the family derives from "the cultural assumptions and premises generally used and understood in the group." Duncan implies that the behavior is familiar to other families of workers, that is, it is "generic" to their assumptions and premises, but it is not necessarily practiced by them. Yet, in my opinion, he still has the task as an anthropologist of ascertaining what behavior is generally shared and approved of and what behavior is considered to be undesirable or deviant. He must also establish empirically whether or not the cultural assumptions and premises are indeed shared by the mill workers.

The anthropologist who studies his own culture is faced with the special problem of publishing results that will be read by those whom he has studied, as well as by a larger audience. Such publication invariably affects his relationships with the group studied and has consequences for follow-up research. No matter how hard the anthropologist may try, disguising the group and the individuals studied is in fact very difficult to accomplish. Thus, those of us who studied the town of "Kent" gave this community a pseudonym and changed the names of persons reported on in the studies. Nevertheless, a number of those in the town were able to see through the disguises. After my study was published (1958), friends in the mill village section invited me to return for a visit. But they advised me to bring my gun, saying, "it won't be for hunting rabbits either." In another example, publication of the study of a small town in upper New York state (Vidich and Bensman 1958) brought forth this reaction in a newspaper report:

> The people of the Village [Springdale] waited quite a while to get even with Art Vidich who wrote a Peyton Place-type book about their town.
> The featured float of the annual 4th of July parade followed an authentic copy of the jacket of the book, SMALL TOWN IN MASS SOCIETY, done large-scale. . . . Following the book cover came residents of [Springdale], riding masked in cars labeled with the fictitious names given them in the book.
> But the payoff was the final scene, a manure-spreader filled with very rich barnyard fertilizer, over which was bending an effigy with a sign around its neck, 'The Author.'[4]

Such difficulties resulting from publication are not peculiar to *in vivo* studies, for other disciplines also face this problem in publishing research on America. However, *in vivo* studies are especially subject to this problem, since they are more intimate and are limited to relatively small, identifiable groups.

Where can anthropological studies in the South go from here? First, there can be a continuation of the two types of research presented in this volume, namely studies of small groups and of specific cultural patterns that appear to characterize the region as a whole.[5] Presumably these kinds of research would be carried out largely as they are now, by interested individuals who can secure financial support. While such studies would be sharply limited in size and confined largely to description and analysis, they would be nonetheless valuable in increasing knowledge about the regional subculture. We are reminded that however large the society being studied, there is always social interaction in small groups reflecting patterns of the society, and that, paradoxically, "only the most intensive studies of very limited areas of social life will make the most extensive comparative work possible" (Frankenberg 1966:149). At the same time, small-scale, individualistic, uncoordinated studies have obvious limitations in the generalizations they can reach and in the research techniques and strategies they can produce.

Another approach is to have teams of anthropologists use entire communities as the object of research. Arensberg contends that communities are the natural settings for *in vivo* study (1961), and Wissler, in his "Foreword" to the Lynds' *Middletown* some forty years ago, said, "Whatever else a social phenomenon is, it is a community affair" (1929:vi). I agree, for it is in the community that the business of life is largely carried on. It is there where parents begin the process of enculturation in their children, where schools continue the process in formal education, where churches and synagogues nourish religious belief and practice, where most occupational, political, and recreational activities are carried out. Such activities extend beyond the bounds of the community, to be sure, but it can be argued that their major focus is in the community, which Arensberg has termed the context "made up of natural and full human cooperative living, of living intergenerational and intersexual relationships, of ongoing cultural and interfamilial communication and transmission" (1954:120). Communities, then, are the units that provide the closest approximations to microcosms of the region and of the larger society. They therefore offer the most suitable settings for holistic study, far more so than the smaller groups within them.

I have previously discussed specific proposals for anthropological study of communities in the American South (1967), and I will summarize and add to those proposals here. What is needed, I feel, is to select several communities for systematic, long-range study. Although there have been a number of anthropological studies of American communities in the past,[6] including some in the South, there has been only one attempt at a systematic, interrelated study. This is the one undertaken by John Gillin and the Institute for Research in Social Science at the University of North Carolina in the late 1940s.[7] The number of communities studied, the particular ones studied, and the extent of detail in the studies done would, of course, depend on how much money is available and whether university departments of anthropology would be interested in organizing such research. If enough communities could be studied to make generalizations about the region valid, then the characteristics of the regional subculture could be ascertained. Regardless of how many communities might be selected for study, the content of the studies could follow this sequence. Initial, or base-line, studies would describe the major patterns of behavior, belief, and attitudes found in each community. Comparison among the communities could indicate the extent of similarity and variation in what is assumed to be a regional subculture.

After initial studies have been made, periodic, or time-interval studies could be utilized to measure socio-cultural change in the communities.[8] If, in the communities studied, family and kinship ties are still found to be among the special value emphases, as Gillin and Murphy (1951) reported earlier, time-interval studies could show what happens to these ties as movement toward the urbanization and standardization of American culture continues. These and other studies, done over a period of time and *in community context*, could contribute a gread deal to our knowledge of how change takes place. Many of the studies in this volume would lend themselves to time-interval research; for example, such research could find out what happens to Newton's peasant settlements as urbanization increases, how Stanton's Houma Indians adjust their self-identify if they are absorbed by the larger society, what happens to Harper's Irish Travelers as their traditional bases of support and separateness change. However, doing these studies in full community context would not be possible until the community setting for each of these groups had been delineated.

Research on Southern communities could also provide for the testing of generalizations about culture and for the generation of additional hypotheses. For example, tests for the normative theory of racial prejudice (Westie 1964) could be undertaken. This theory is sometimes contrasted to psychological theories like the scapegoat theory (that prejudice is a function of frustration and aggression) or the authoritarian personality or psychological syndrome theory (that prejudice is the function of a fascistic or authoritarian personality make-up). The normative theory of prejudice assumes that prejudice is a cultural matter, a part of the normative order in the society in which it occurs. In this sense prejudice is conceived to be normal in that it has been acquired by most of those growing up in society, as have language and other aspects of culture. Prejudice, then, is assumed to be an aspect of the society's system of norms defining what ought to be, particularly in regard to how the individual members of the society ought to evaluate and interact with particular groups within and outside the society. In such a normative system both the person without prejudice and the person with excessive prejudice would be deviants. In testing this theory in the communities under study, the anthropologist would first delineate the patterning of prejudice, seeing to what extent it varied by social characteristics within each community and how it varied among the communities themselves. He could then determine if the norms were related to the patterning of prejudice and to variations in the patterning.

Developing base-line, time-interval, theory-testing studies in Southern communities is admittedly an ambitious program. Kimball (1955) has reminded us of what an enormous, time-consuming undertaking the study even of small communities is. Also, most anthropological community research has been in relatively small towns, and we still have much to learn about what is required for anthropological study of large cities.[9] Yet, I am convinced that such systematic, co-operative, long-term research is necessary if anthropology is to make its full contribution to the understanding of American culture. The enormity of the task could be allayed somewhat by working with social scientists from other fields, something Gillin has often advocated (1967:305). Also, some sort of institute for directing and coordinating such studies of the South, for example the Center for Southern Studies at Duke University, would be most helpful.

In his presidential address before the American Anthropological Association in 1965, Alexander Spoehr spoke about the importance of regional study in anthropology. Although he used as his example Oceania and did not speak about the United States or the South, I think that what he had to say is germane to my proposal for studying the American South:

We cannot get along without regional specialization, so long as empirical observation is the basis of archeology and ethnography. The problem of achieving maximum results is at least partly one of examining what a given region has to offer. Regions differ in their potentialities for fruitful work, and it may well be that in some, the major opportunities already have been exploited. We must spend more time in identifying these varying potentialities (1966:637).

I am convinced that anthropological study of the American South as a regional subculture of the United States offers tremendous potentialities for fruitful work.

## NOTES

1. For additional discussions of these problems, see Arensberg (1954; 1961), Colson (1967), Gillin (1949; 1957), Kimball (1955), and Mitchell (1967).
2. For fieldwork experiences of anthropologists, including the problem of acceptance, see Spindler (1970).
3. The complications of translation become particularly acute in cross-cultural research, as I discovered in comparing race-awareness and racial attitudes of Americans and Hong Kong Chinese (Morland 1969; Morland and Williams 1969). The questions that had been used with Americans were translated into Chinese by my 19 Chinese students in a social anthropology class at the Chinese University of Hong Kong. I then asked Chinese colleagues who knew English well to translate the Chinese back into English. Significant differences from the original English appeared, so it was necessary for my students to work out these differences before arriving at a satisfactory translation.
4. Quoted in an editorial, "Freedom and Responsibility in Research: the 'Springdale' Case," *Human Organization,* 17:1-2.
5. Studies of "streetcorner" men by Whyte (1955) and Liebow (1967) are examples of research on small groups in large cities. See van Velsen (1967) and Kimball and Pearsall (1955) for other approaches to delimitation.
6. Most of these are listed in Mandelbaum, *et al.* (1961:265-269).
7. Called "Field Studies in the Modern Culture of the South." Publications include Gillin and Murphy (1951), Rubin (1951), Lewis (1955), Morland (1958).
8. For one such time-interval study, see Morland (1964).
9. Developments in the field of urban anthropology can be helpful with this problem. See, for example, Eddy (1968).

## REFERENCES

Arensberg, Conrad M., 1954. The Community-Study Method. *American Journal of Sociology* 60:109-124.

--------------------------- 1955. American Communities. *American Anthropologist* 57:1143-1162.

--------------------------- 1961. The Community as Object and as Sample. *American Anthropologist* 63:241-264.

Colson, Elizabeth, 1967. The Intensive Study of Small Sample Communities. In *The Craft of Social Anthropology*, A. L. Epstein, ed. (London: Tavistock), pp. 3-15.

Frankenberg, Ronald, 1966. British Community Studies: Problems of Synthesis. In *The Social Anthropology of Complex Societies*, Michael Banton, ed. (New York: Praeger), pp. 123-149.

Eddy, Elizabeth M., ed., 1968. *Urban Anthropology: Research Perspectives and Strategies*, Southern Anthropological Society Proceedings, No. 2 (Athens, Georgia: University of Georgia Press).

Gillin, John, 1949. Methodological Problems in the Anthropological Study of Modern Cultures. *American Anthropologist* 51:392-399.

_____ 1957. The Application of Anthropological Knowledge to Modern Mass Society: An Anthropologist's View. *Human Organization* 15:24-29.

_____ 1967. More Complex Cultures for Anthropologists. *American Anthropologist* 69:301-305.

Gillin, John and Emmett J. Murphy, 1951. Notes on Southern Culture Patterns. *Social Forces* 29:422-432.

Gluckman, Max and Fred Eggan, 1966. Introduction. In *The Social Anthropology of Complex Societies*, Michael Banton, ed. (New York: Praeger), pp. xi-xliii.

Herskovits, Melville J., 1955. *Cultural Anthropology* (New York: Knopf).

Kimball, Solon T., 1955. Problems of Studying American Culture. *American Anthropologist* 57:1131-1142.

Kimball, Solon T. and Marion Pearsall, 1955. Event Analysis as an Approach to Community Study. *Social Forces* 34:58-63.

Lantis, Margaret, 1955. Introduction: The U.S.A. as Anthropologists See It. *American Anthropologist* 57:1113-1120.

Lewis, Hylan, 1955. *Blackways of Kent* (Chapel Hill: University of North Carolina Press).

Liebow, Elliott, 1967. *Tally's Corner* (Boston: Little, Brown).

Mandelbaum, David G., 1953. On the Study of National Character. *American Anthropologist* 55:174-187.

Mandelbaum, David G., Gabriel W. Lasker, and Ethel M. Albert, eds., 1963. *Resources for the Teaching of Anthropology*, Memoir 95 of the American Anthropological Association.

Mead, Margaret, 1949. *Male and Female* (New York: Morrow).

_____ 1953. National Character. In *Anthropology Today: An Encyclopedic Inventory*, prepared under the chairmanship of A. L. Kroeber (Chicago: University of Chicago Press), pp. 642-667.

Mitchell, J. Clyde, 1967. On Quantification in Social Anthropology. In *The Craft of Social Anthropology*, A. L. Epstein, ed. (London: Tavistock), pp. 17-45.

Morland, J. Kenneth, 1958. *Millways of Kent* (Chapel Hill: University of North Carolina Press).

——————— 1964. Kent Revisited: Blue-Collar Aspirations and Achievement. In *Blue-Collar World*, A. B. Shostak and W. Gomberg, eds. (Englewood Cliffs, N. J.: Prentice-Hall), pp. 134-143.

——————— 1967. Anthropology and the Study of Culture, Society, and Community in the South. In *Perspectives on the South*, Edgar T. Thompson, ed. (Durham: Duke University Press), pp. 124-145.

——————— 1969. Race Awareness among American and Hong Kong Chinese Children. *American Journal of Sociology* 75:360-374.

Morland, J. Kenneth and John E. Williams, 1969. Cross-Cultural Measurement of Racial and Ethnic Attitudes by the Semantic Differential. *Social Forces* 48:107-112.

Rubin, Morton, 1951. *Plantation County* (Chapel Hill: University of North Carolina Press).

Spindler, George D., ed. 1970. *Being an Anthropologist: Fieldwork in Eleven Cultures* (New York: Holt, Rinehart, Winston).

Spoehr, Alexander, 1966. The Part and the Whole: Reflections on the Study of a Region. *American Anthropologist* 68:629-640.

van Velsen, J., 1967. The Extended-case Method and Situational Analysis. In *The Craft of Social Anthropology*, A. L. Epstein, ed. (London: Tavistock), pp. 129-149.

Vidich, Arthur J. and Joseph Bensman, 1958. *Small Town in Mass Society* (Princeton, N. J.: Princeton University Press).

Westie, Frank R., 1964. Race and Ethnic Relations. In *Handbook of Modern Sociology*, R. E. L. Faris, ed. (Chicago: Rand McNally), pp. 576-618.

White, Leslie A., 1965. Anthropology 1964: Retrospect and Prospect. *American Anthropologist* 67:629-637.

Whyte, William Foote, 1955. *Street-Corner Society*, Revised Edition (Chicago: University of Chicago Press).

Wissler, Clark, 1929. Foreword. In *Middletown: A Study in Contemporary American Culture*, by Robert S. Lynd and Helen M. Lynd (New York: Harcourt, Brace), pp. v-vii.

# The Contributors

*Christopher Crocker* is associate professor of anthropology at Duke University. He has done field work among the Eastern Bororo Indians of Brazil. His main professional specializations are symbolic behavior, South American ethnography, and kinship systems.

*Ronald J. Duncan* is assistant professor in the Department of Anthropology and in the School of Urban Life at Georgia State University. He has done field work in Mexico and in black and white communities in the United States. He is currently doing research on cultural influences on social change in urban communities in the United States. His theoretical interests are applied anthropology, culture theory and the individual, the personal experience of culture, and descriptive techniques in ethnography.

*John Gordon* is a graduate student in social anthropology at Harvard University. He plans to do field work in eastern Indonesia.

*Jared Harper* is instructor of anthropology in the Department of Sociology and Anthropology at Virginia Commonwealth University. He has done field work among Negroes and Irish Travelers in North Carolina and South Carolina. Currently he is working on a sociolinguistic study of soul lingo.

*H. Eugene Hodges* is a sociologist in the Georgia Department of Public Health, Division of Mental Health. His areas of interest are in the sociology of deviance and the sociology of mental health. He has done field work in the Southeastern United States on the Southern fundamentalist belief system and popular explanations of the causes of mental deviance.

*Edward E. Knipe* is assistant professor in the Department of Sociology and Anthropology at Virginia Commonwealth University. His primary interests are theoretical anthropology, urban anthropology, and socio-technical change.

*Helen M. Lewis* is assistant professor of sociology and anthropology at Clinch Valley College of the University of Virginia. Her main interests are in the Southern Appalachians, especially the coal mining regions. She has carried out research on the family structure of coal mining families and on changes in coal mining communities.

*J. Kenneth Morland* is chairman of the Department of Sociology and Anthropology at Randolph-Macon Woman's College. Most of his field work has been in the American South, but he has also done studies in New England and in Hong Kong. His current interest is in anthropological studies of complex societies, particularly in comparative studies of racial attitudes, connotations of color, and race awareness in young children. Among his publications is *Millways of Kent*, a study of mill village life in a Southern town.

*Milton B. Newton, Jr.* is assistant professor of geography in the Department of Geography and Anthropology, Louisiana State University. His main interest is in settlement geography approached from the cultural point of view; his main region of interest is the South. Other interests include the history of the frontier and settlement archeology.

*William L. Partridge* is a graduate student at the University of Florida in Gainesville. His particular field of interest is urban areas and the anthropology of complex societies.

*James L. Peacock* is associate professor and associate chairman in the Department of Anthropology, University of North Carolina, Chapel Hill. He has done field work in Singapore and Indonesia. His main interest is in the ideological dimension of modernization. Most recently he has been investigating the psycho-social ramifications of Muslim reformation movements in Southeast Asia.

*Helen Phillips Keber* is a graduate student in the Department of Anthropology at the University of North Carolina, Chapel Hill. Her interests include medical and symbolic anthropology, revitalization movements, and modernization. She is currently doing dissertation research on black divine healing.

*Robert Sayers* is currently a graduate student in the Department of Anthropology at the University of Arizona. His topical interests are several: folklife studies in rural areas of the United States, craft technologies, cultural change, and North American Indians. He has done field work in various of the Southeastern states. Most recently he has been interested in Southern Athapaskan ethnology.

*Max E. Stanton* is a Ph.D. candidate at the University of Oregon who is presently a visiting instructor of anthropology in the Department of Anthropology at Southwestern at Memphis. He has done field work among the Crow Indians and the Houma Indians. His topical interests are contemporary culture change among the North American Indians and among the Polynesians and adjacent peoples of Oceania. He is currently investigating sociocultural change among the urban Samoan immigrants in California and New Zealand.

# Southern Anthropological
# Society Proceedings

Thomas Weaver (ed.), *Essays on Medical Anthropology*, 1968, No. 1. $3.00

Elizabeth M. Eddy (ed.), *Urban Anthropology: Research Perspectives and Strategies*, 1968, No. 2. $3.00

Stephen A. Tyler (ed.), *Concepts and Assumptions in Contemporary Anthropology*, 1969, No. 3. $3.00

J. Kenneth Morland (ed.), *The Not So Solid South: Anthropological Studies in a Regional Subculture*, 1971, No. 4. $3.75

Charles Hudson (ed.), *Red, White, and Black: Symposium on Indians in the Old South*, 1971, No. 5. $3.75